VEENA TRADITION IN INDIAN MUSIC

VEENA TRADITION IN INDIAN MUSIC

L. ANNAPOORNA, *Secretary*
SRISHTI,
Indian Music Research Foundation,
Madurai

KANISHKA PUBLISHERS, DISTRIBUTORS
NEW DELHI-110002

KANISHKA PUBLISHERS, DISTRIBUTORS
4697/5-21A, Ansari Road, Daryaganj
New Delhi -110 002
Phones : 2327 0497, 2328 8285
Fax : 011-2328 8285
E-mail : kanishka_publishing@yahoo.co.in

First Published: 1996
Second Edition: 2012

ISBN: 978-81-7391-140-1

PRINTED IN INDIA

Published by Madan Sachdeva for Kanishka Publishers, Distributors, 4697/5-21A, Ansari Road, Daryaganj, New Delhi-110 002, Typeset by Sunshine Graphics, Delhi, and Printed at Rajdhani Printers, Delhi.

ACKNOWLEDGEMENTS

I am thankful to Dr. M. HARIHARAN my guide for advising me to work on this interesting study.

I am also beholden to my Alma-mater Sri Sathguru Sangeetha Vidyalayam for giving me facilities to work on this topic during my Master's degree programme.

I am also grateful to all the Vidwans and Vidushis for their instant and personal help extended to me during my preliminary interviews and recording sessions.

I am also thankful to my teachers both at my Alma-mater and outside for their constant inspiration.

I am also extremely thankful to M/s Kanishka Publishers, Distributors, New Delhi for readily agreeing to include this book in their publication schedule.

PROLOGUE

Having undergone training for a few of five years I was abie to conceive upon the idea of identifying the fact that, in the realm of Veena different styles and techniques did exist. Several natural constraints and limitations did not give me an opportunity to know the various styles that was in vogue. The main reason for this lack of understanding was also because of the fact that my circumstances of learning within the academic curriculum was exposed to different and varied styles of teaching. This lacuna of my understanding the techniques and style—a basic essential knowledge required for a post-graduate student—was realised only when I happened to listen to a series of live concerts in Veena.

At this juncture my quest for knowing more about the various styles started sprouting up and the urge to fulfill the idea somehow or other took shape. Fortunately the compulsory completion of the Dissertation paper, became more useful and handy to serve this purpose.

When I commenced forming ideas to the ways and means of collecting data on 'Studying the various styles of Vainikas' I was forced to confront with the truth that the existing styles had its basic roots in the styles of old masters. And unfortunately I had no means to listen to these old masters. Again my ambition to take up this topic, became still more difficult.

As luck would have it in one of my preliminary discussions with a leading Vainika I was made to understand that a tradition has nothing to do with styles or technique and each Vainika only transferred his or her knowledge to their next generation of progenies or disciples. It was the individual technique and style that is prominently displayed in one's rendering. In other words the much commonly used term 'bani' is often wrongly understood to denote a particular style or technique instead of the age-old tradition.

Still my doubts on the original identity of the 'bani' of old masters was an unfulfilled affair. Therefore, my confusion on linking the basic source tradition of the contemporary Vainikas *vis-a-vis* old masters always remained unaccountable and puzzled one. In other words, to speak of a tradition of Karaikudi or Veena Dhanammal or Thanjavur School being continued or transferred to their progenies of disciples was respectively an exaggerated affair far from truth.

In order to get a first hand information I initially adopted the idea of distinguishing if at all any particular style or technique within the precincts of my college teaching existed. But I failed to identify any. On the other hand when I tried to analyse the fingering or plucking techniques or for that matter the reckoning of the taala strings, I succeeded in distinguishing identical phenomena in each individual.

These two factors had its effect both on the positive and negative aspects. Positive in the sense that my ambition to study and analyse the various styles started taking fruition. The negative sense was that it made me aberrant in the learning process. In other words, different teachers concurrently infusing their different styles to me at the same time was like drifting on a boat without a place to anchor in on land. My hidden ambition to specialise on this beautiful instrument to a greater extent became difficult due to the constraints.

Coming to the subject matter of the study, as I said earlier my confusion within myself became persistent because of my over enthusiasm to identify the much-talked-about different styles. At the same time the knowledge gained within the short period of my course curriculum also made me think twice before embarking upon this sensitive, tricky, controversial and different areas of study.

I would also like to point out that while Dr. T. Visvanathan (Wesleyan University in U.S.) concluded a study on different vocal styles and Dr. L. Sankar at the same University made an indepth study of different violin styles—both of them without specifying on any particular school, Dr. K.S. Subramaniam (University of Madras) also at the same University recently concluded a research study on the 'South Indian Veena Tradition and Individual Style (Musicians' family, history, voice and instrument, analysis, inventive notation)'. These and other such studies also helped me to proceed further on this subject on a positive note in my mind.

Before I started collecting data, I did glance through some of the reference sources—both books and journals—which discussed in detail on the fretting system of the Veena. For instance the literature on Raghunatha Nayak's system of fretting and Sarngadeva's *Sangitaratnakara* on fingering and plucking methods were highly useful. This I did with the main intention to find out (as mentioned earlier) if at all any different pattens of styles could be identified because of the varying systems of fretting and plucking. I also made up my mind to attend to some Live and Radio concerts of some of the Vidwans on whose styles I decided to study later on. The foremost problem of successfully completing the study in a systematic way was also ever lingering and bothering me.

The concerts that I attended included Ms. Chittibabu, Gayatri, Doreswami Iyengar, Sivanandham, Balachandar, Pichumani, Seshagopalan, Kalpakam Swaminathan, etc. But my lack of direct or indirect knowledge on the Veena-Style of the Karaikudi Brothers, Veena Dhanammal and Devakottai Narayana Iyengar was always nagging me.

With this mind-set and short musical background I decided upon to take up the present study on 'Vainikas : Their Tradition and Styles'.

At the same time, as I said earlier in my inner mind I had already visualised the arduous task that lay ahead of me on the immensity of the subject that I was going to deal with.

As second phase of my data collection I had the fortunate opportunity of personally meeting several top Vainikas of the decade and with the help of taped interviews with them I was able to collect authentic and first hand information on their assiduous application of own styles and techniques.

Another fortunate and pleasant thing is that most of the Vainikas whom I met and interviewed expressed their utmost interest and support in the subject of study and in fact this further strengthened latently hidden enthusiasm.

Before I could conclude my several notes of experience and inner most expression I must thank my revered teachers (in the Veena Department of College) for initiating me into the ocean of music through my favourite medium of expression—The VEENA. Their inspiration was also of the cause that led me to realise the importance and voluminous depth of the present subject.

Due to my lack of full and through exposure to the subject, there are every chance that one might find fault with the handling of the whole subject. To offset this remark I have decided to analyse and make it more evident with the help of recorded cassettes.

In the significant chapter on 'Analysis of the Styles of Contemporary Vainikas' I have rightly pointed out at least three identifiable individual techniques of each Vainika. For an easy following of the verbal analysis illustrated in the cassette by me I have also provided a script (vide the script for audiography) in the Dissertation. But still whatever is said will always be incomplete in the absence of a practical demonstration. To suffice this idea I have myself given in the cassette a small illustration of the techniques that I have understood. The main objective of my illustration is to prove that the Analysis forms completely my own interpretation on which others may or may not agree.

L. ANNAPOORNA

CONTENTS

1

INTRODUCTION

In the history of Indian Music, the word 'Veena' seems to have been used as a general term to denote any stringed instruments. Literary materials undoubtedly help us to gather lot of information but, it still seems inadequate to enable one to arrive at a precise conclusion on the evolution of this instrument. In fact, the description of Sarngadeva in his *Sangita Ratnakara* only gets us closer to the present day structure of the Veena. Nevertheless, the innumerable references in sculpture, painting, etc. are not suggested to be ignored. Even the popular experiment of Bharata, on the Dhruva and Chala Veenas do not throw any idea on the structure and shape of the instrument as such.

When the concert pattern set in, the importance of Veena at first gained currency over vocal music. The reason for this was the existence of orchestral music (Vadyabrinda). This established that a person has to be a master of the instrument that he/she handled to give solo performances so as to gain universal recognition.

Several music treatises also speak of the various aspects of Veena on the construction, number of strings, tuning methods, materials to be used and so on, but unfortunately the practical application along with the adaptation of the technique, have not been made easily understandable. In this respect, Govinda Dikshitar, Ramamatya and Venkatamakhi have made sincere attempts to fill up the above lacuna.

The tradition set by Govinda Dikshitar was put to practice by the illustrious Muthuswamy Dikshitar—a divine Veena player—who imbibed the Veena, or in other words, instrumental technique into vocal music. His brother Baluswamy Dikshitar, himself a Veena player, Tyagaraja's two foremost disciples—Veena Kuppiar and Umayalpuram Krishna Bhagavatar were known to have gained complete mastery over this instrument.

Other Vainikas who followed them establishing a style of their own included :

1. Veena Kalahastiayya
2. Sonti Venkataramanaiah
3. Pachimiriyam Adippaiah
4. Veena Subbiah
5. Veena Subbukuttiayya
6. Ramaswamyayya
7. Pallavi Gopalayya
8. Chikka Othappayya
9. Varahappiar
10. Veena Appiah
11. Veena Sambiah
12. Veena Seshanna
13. Veena Subbanna
14. Venkataramanadas
15. Sangameswara Sastri
16. Veena Venkatagiriappa
17. Veena Karigirirao
18. Karaikudi Subbarama Iyer
19. Karaikudi Sambasiva Iyer
20. Veena Dhanammal
21. Devakkottai Narayana Iyengar
22. Emani Sankara Sastri

The contemporary Vainikas with their new innovative ideas and inspirations derived from the earlier stalwarts infused new techniques and ideas, thereby, establishing a new style and technique of their own. Some of them are:

1. Padma Bhushan late Sri S. Balachandar
2. Padma Sri Chitti Babu

3. Sangita Kalanidhi Padma Bhushan Dr. V. Doreswamy Iyengar
4. Kalaimamani Srimati E. Gayatri
5. Kalaimamani Srimati Kalpakam Swaminathan
6. Sangita Kalanidhi Padma Bhushan Sri K.S. Narayanaswamy
7. Kalaimamani Sri R. Pichumani
8. Kalaimamani Rajeswari Padmanabhan
9. Kalaimamani Ranganayaki Rajagopalan
10. Kalaimamani Srimati Sarada
11. Sangita Kalanidhi Sri K.P. Sivanandham
12. Kalaimamani Sri T.N. Seshigopalan
13. Nadajothi Sri R.K. Suryanarayana and so on.

There is no denying the fact that several other Vainikas not mentioned here did not contribute in establishing an identity of their own in the field of Veena-technique.

2

CONCERT TRADITION

1. Ancient System

Ancient works on music in Sanskrit and Tamil deal elaborately with raaga aalaapana. In the *Sangita Ratnakara*, aalaapana is dealt with at great length as consisting of several stages like Akshiptika, Vidaari and Makarini. It mentions rupakalapti in which a portion of song is taken up for improvisation. This is obviously what is called niraval now-a-days. Tamil works like the *Pancha Marabu* also deal with aalati. There are three kinds of aalati : 1. Pan-aalati 2. nira-aalati and 3. kaatt-aalati.

Pan-aalati is aalaapana of the raaga, nira-aalati is improvisation of the text of the song and kaatt-aalati is performed to the accompaniment of the dance. The latter two are performed in a rhythmic set up.

Considering the pattern of naadaswaram performances 50 years ago, it may be speculated that vocal performances were conducted along the same lines *i.e.* elaborate aalaapana of a particular raaga followed by taanam and pallavi, after which a few pieces were sung.

Therefore, a concert may be defined as a performance by two or more musicians, vocal, instrumental, or both before an audience. Bharata in his *Naatyasaastra* says that music concerts could be arranged on the following occasions:

1. at coronations
2. at weddings

3. during festivals both household and at the temples.

Our Puraanaas make many references to music and musicians. Two incidents may be mentioned here as illustrative of the fact that the spirit of competition existed in the world of music.

In the *Tiruvilaiyaadal Puraanam* there is an episode of a musician by name Emanaathan coming to the Paandya kingdom to challenge the court musicians, Banabhadran of the Paandya court was afraid to face the northerner in the contest. Lord Siva, in order to save his devotee from ignominy took the form of the wood-cutter, and carrying the bundle of firewood on this head went to the residence of Emanaathan and began to sing the pan Sasdari. Emanaathan came out, thrilled by the music and asked him who he was.

An episode in the *Periapuraanam* is a very interesting one. Tirugnaana Sambandaar had Tiruneelakanta Yaazhpaanar for yaazh accompaniment. Once the relatives of the latter declared that the child's singing was rendered attractive only because of the yaazh accompaniment of their kinsman. This wounded the feelings of the Paanar who rushed to young Sambandar and said, "Please sing today in such a way as to make it impossible for me to accompany it on the yaazh. That will teach my relatives a lesson". Accordingly Sambandar sang the verse 'Madhar Madapidiyin'. The Paanar could not reproduce it in his yaazh. Now the artist in him came to the fore and he was very sorry and dejected about not being able to play the tune. Frustrated, he wanted to break the instrument. Sambandar stopped him and said, "Any voice is God-given whereas your instrument is man-made. The instrument will have its own limitations. Please play within those limits". The melody subsequently came to be known as yaazhmuripan (yaazh breaker).

The *Silappadikaaram* described the music that accompanied the dance of Madhavi before the Chola king Karikaala. The flute leads the music. Yaazh (harp), tannumai (drum) and amantirikai (idakkai) follow it closely. The 'Adiyaarkku Nallaar' commentary speaks of musical instruments under three categories.

1. Instruments which accompany vocal music (Gitaanugam)
2. Instruments which accompany dance (Nrittaanugam)
3. Instruments which accompany both (Ubhayaanugam)

The *Silapadikaaram* of Ilangovadigal contains a number of songs like Kaanalvari sung by Kovalan and Maadhavi to the accompaniment of the yaazh, Kuravai Paadal sung by the cowherd women in Mullai Pan (Mohanam), and the Vettuva vari songs sung by huntsmen. Though the texts of the songs are available we have no clues as to how they were sung in those times.

The Tamil *Tevaaram* hymns of Appar, Sambandar and Sundarar (7th and 8th century A.D.) have fortunately been handed down to this day thanks to the Chola king Raaja Raaja I who ordained that these songs be sung in all Saivite temples. Thus we have specimens of the music which is more than ten centuries old. But these hymns were sung by a congregation of musicians called Oduvaars (Tevaara Gosti) and so, excepting for the Tiruthandaham and Tiruvirutham, there was no scope for improvisation. It was more or less the equivalent of the Gregorian chant, the church music of the West.

Between the 8th and 15th centuries which saw the advent of Annamaachaarya (Telugu), Purandara Daas (Kannada) and Arunagirinaathar (Tamil), the Tiruvisaippa of Kandaraditta Thevar and the Tirupallaandu of Senthan Amudhaanar are the only Tamil compositions worth mentioning.

It must be pointed out that the Vaishnavite Aalwaars also composed 4000 exquisite Tamil hymns set to pans like the Tevaaram. Their music is lost, as the chanting of the hymns in temples had been modelled after the vedic chant.

From the 15th century onward Thanjavur came under the sway of the Telugu Naayaks and later the Marathaa rulers. Tamil lost its exalted place as the Telugu language came to be patronised by the Naayaks. It was during Vijayaraaghava Naayak's time that the great Kshetragnya composed hundreds of his padamas in Telugu.

Narayana Tirtha, another Telugu who migrated from Andhra to Varahur composed his 'Krishna Leela Tarangini' in Sanskrit. Tyagaraja whose ancestors had migrated from Andhra to Tiruvaiyaaru composed hundreds of songs in Telugu, his mother-tongue. The Thanjavur court patronised about 360 musicians. Most of them were of Telugu origin. Pachimiriam Adippaiah, the author of the *Bhiravi varnam* (the guru of Syama Sastri) and Pallavi Gopaaliah had honoured places in the Thanjavur court. Sonti Venkata Subbiah, the father of Sonti Venkataramanaiah (the guru of Tyagaraja) was the chief court musician. It is said that each of the musicians had to perform on one day in the year. The Sangita Mahal attached to the Thanjavur Palace was the venue for such concerts.

Tyagaraja's disciple Walajapet Venkatarama Bhagavathar has mentioned the concert given by Tyagaraja before his guru. He reports that Tyagaraja performed the aalaapana of Bilahari and then sang his own song 'Dorakuna' following it up with niraal and kalpanaa swaras in one of the charanams.

It may be mentioned that Pachimiriam Adippaiah is believed to have established the practice of pallavi singing. The pallavi consists of a text with just a few words fixed in a rhythmic set up in a particular taala and a particular raaga and the musician is expected to improvise on it. The word "Pallavi" itself is said to represent 'pa' meaning 'pada' or words, 'la' standing for 'laya' or rhythmic set up and 'vi' representing 'vinyaasam' or elaboration.

Before the compositions of the Trinity gained wide popularity our music was marked by raaga praadhaanya, importance being given to the expansion of the melodic framework, very much like the North Indian music of today. Lyrics were given importance only in the Bhajana Saṃpradaaya. Such a tradition naturally gave prominence to the hours long elaboration of the raagam, taanam and pallavi. The fact that the term pallavi was prefixed to the names of great vidwans like Gopala Iyer, Sesha Iyer, Narasimha Iyer, etc. tells us that this was the most important part of a concert, the test of a musician worth.

The Bhajana tradition which got established in the 15th century in Tamil Nadu gradually began to use Chinnaiah's compositions, the ashtapadis of Jayadeva the tarangams of Narayana Tirtha and the devotional songs of Bhadrachala Ramadas. It may be pointed out that there were recitals exclusively of the *Tiruppugazh* songs of Arunagirinaathar as also of the Ramanataka kirtanas of Arunaachala Kavi. In these concerts there was practically no scope for improvisation. Even padams and jaavali figured exclusively in some concerts.

It may be interesting to note that flute and the yaazh were used to provide accompaniment to vocal music. The Veena and the jalatarangam were also used in this manner. But after the advent of violin in the early part of the 19th century all the other instruments used for accompaniment were given up and the violin began to be main instrument for accompaniment.

Treatises like *Sangita Ratnakara* deal profusely with several types of compositions (Prabandhas) like Kaivara Prabandha, Sriranga Prabandha and Umatilaka Prabandha. It passes ones understanding how these Prabandhas could have been used in those times.

The Tamil word for concert is 'cutcheri' though this word also refers to a court or an office. Sometimes the word melaa is also used. This word is derived from the root 'mil' (coming together). The naadaswaram troupe consisting of two naadaswarams, ottu (drone), cymbals and thavil is referred to as periamelam and the dance troupe consisting the danseuse, nattuvanaar, maddalam player, tutti (drone), flute, clarinet, etc. is referred to as chinna melam.

We speak of melam kattudal which is the forging of a rapport between the performer and the listener. The prologue in a dance performance, sung for the creation of the right atmosphere, is called melapraapti.

2. Medieval System

The word 'Tradition' connotes the sum total of observances and practices as they come down in human history, in the aspect of man's mental and social activities such as literature, art, religion and philosophy. Each generation takes up the heritage of its distant and immediate past and perforce moulds it to the needs, temperaments and capacities of its own time. Therefore, tradition cannot be a dead fossil of the past, but it is a continuity of it will cease to have a living quality about it. Its validity is proven by the discovery of its moorings in the early ages of human history.

Modern classical concert music is an instance in point. The limbs and parts which go to make up the present day concert are the growth of such basic elements and components that were born even as early as a thousand years ago. To give a few instances, the raaga, the soul of our music is a lyrical and historical corrollary of a development from "jatis", dating from 7th or 8th century A.D. Swara prastaara seems to have existed as early or even earlier than the 13th century A.D. Both the *Sangita Ratnakara* of Sarngadeva and the later *Ragavibodha* mention swara varisais or alankaaras about sixty in number which are quite aesthetic and interesting, judged even by modern standards.

"Kootatanam" as opposed to "Suddhasadhanam" is swara prastaara in vakra order. Taanam singing of the modern type in which raaga phrases are sung to madhyama kaala with specified Sied letters or aksharas, seems to be only 300 to 400 years old. Again pallavi singing has been hinted at and vaguely described in the words "Roopaka Aalapati" in the *Sangita Ratnakara*.

Between the post *Ratnakara* period, about which time, the Indian music system seems to have bifurcated itself into the southern and northern systems and the 18th century, the 72 melakartas with their enormous possibilities for the creation of innumerable janya raagas had been propounded and exploited. The theory of the music of the south had been promulgated in all its elaborateness and detail Purandara Daasa had laid secure foundations of our music with his alankaaram, geetham and suladais, not to speak of thousands of his padas. Lakshana Geethams for many raagas had been composed by Venkatamukhi and others. The ground had been thoroughly prepared for the flowering of men of genius like the South Indian Trinity who appeared in the firmament of music and flooded our continent with the light of their celestial compositions. The Kriti in its embryo form in the *Geetha Govinda* reached adolscence with the Talapaakkam composers followed by Bhadrachala Ramdaas and others and attained its full maturity in the compositions of Sri Tyagaraja, Syama Sastri and Dikshitar periods of private and royal patronage of music have always been rich in producing great composers, and public encouragement, great performers, and public encouragement, great performers. In the pre-Tyagaraja period, concerts were mostly held in the chambers of royalty and zamindars, where only a chosen few were privileged to listen to classical music. The concert then, which lasted for about two hours and more was mainly elaborate raaga singing followed by pallavi. Musical history has it that even contests in such concerts were held in royal concerts. Naadaswaram, the most effective instrument for the propagation of classical music among the masses, on coccasions of royal festivities as also religious and temple utsavas, was the medium through which, large sections of the public got gradually acquainted with many prasiddha raagas and taalas.

Thus it will be seen that all the materials for the structure of modern concerts, barring Kritis were ready in the Tyagaraja period. The early forms of music like tayams, Prabandhas etc., were swept away by the advent of the Kritis. But their spirit continued to live in the varieties of the Kritis produced by the Trinity. Dikshitar's Kritis are Prabandhas in spirit, those of Tyagaraja and Syama Sastri, of kaavya. Kalpanaa Sangita which was till then only confined to raagam and pallavi could now be had through the interpretation of various types of compositions.

From an analysis of the history of our music from very early times up to the 18th century, it will be evident that there had been a progressive, though slow, evolution of music in all its forms which gave nourishment and growth to individual talent, through scientific methods and codification of musical practice and knowledge. Ample opportunities were afforded in private houses of royalty and zamindars for exhibitions of such individual artistic talents. The adaptation of the modern violin, an importation from the West and exploitation of its possibilities as a solo and accompanying medium in a concert came in handy and timely when the concert emerged from the private chambers into the public wing. With the increasing patronage of music by the public and private audiences, musicians were tempted to pursue it as a career. The performer as such had to enlarge his stock and repertoire. Unalloyed interpretative music was found inadequate to meet the increasing demands from the public. The performer has to include recitative portions also in the concert before and after the raagam, taanam and pallavi. The post-Tyagaraja period saw an exuberance of compositions like tillaanas, jaavals etc. which supplied the needs of the performing musicians in this respect. The large volume of compositionss of the Trinity came in at a very strategic and psychological moment. These compositions afforded unprecedented scope for the display of individual talent in the very handling of such pieces as well as in prodiving raaga prologues to the pieces and in the nirayal and swara improvisations which could be introduced during or after the recitation of the piece. They were also of such wide range of variety as could suit the varying musical temperaments and equipments of many talented and gifted musicians, as also various grades of the fast growing public taste for music.

It was in this way that the two major aspects, the determinate and indeterminate (the receptive and the interpretative) became the warp and woof of the texture of the modern concert. The modern concert is a well thought-out and schemed arrangement in the presentation of classical music on both these aspects. The concert could be divided into three segments, (1) the pre-pallavi segment, (2) the raagam, taanam and pallavi and (3) the post-pallavi and comparatively lighter segment. The one which precedes the pallavi is a mixture of recitative and interpretative elements. From the opening varnam, through alternating fast and slow paced Kritis, small raaga prologues to the former and elaborate expositions for the latter, the classical atmosphere gets gradually heightened. It culminates in the second segment, *i.e.* raagam, taanam and pallavi which is the high water-mark of South Indian classical music. It is the peak of the concert. From the raagam, taanam, pallavi, to the end of the performance, there is a gradual watering down of classical music through light classical and light music, so that at the end, even non-classical folk and Hindustani melodies fit with naturalness into the pattern of the concert. Even in the pre-pallavi portion, in the rendering of each piece, the succession of the raagam, Kriti, niraval and swara has a significance. From the raaga to Kriti, from Kriti to niraval and from niraval to swara improvisation, it is a graded, increasing emergence and emphasis of the aspect of laya.

The unique appeal and greatness of our art are owing to its capacity for growth and adaptation, through a long period of time and more so because, men of great genius, through their knowledge and intelligene could have the greatest freedom for the play of both these factors within the framework of tradition. Our system, the most aesthetic, intricate and exalted in the world, is the noblest heritage of man. Our concert tradition has come to stay. It will be good to remind ourselves that all Art is great to the extent that it is informed of the spirit, by the nobility of its content, harmony of its parts and the elegance in its presentation. We should not allow this great heritage to disintegrate into mere and empty aesthetic formalism and uninspired technique and showmanship, which inordinate and indiscriminate commercialisation of any art is likely to bring in its wake.

3. Post-Trinity System

The minimum number of instruments used in a vocal concert would be in addition to the singer, the tambura, the violin and the mridangam. Many concerts include upa pakka vaadyams such as the ghatam and the kanjeeraa. Carnatic music offers a greater variety in instrument ensembles such as the violin, flute, Veena combination, orchestral presentations such as the vaadyavrinda of All India Radio as taalavaadya cutcheris of different kinds of percussion instruments. In addition jugal bandhis featuring instrumentalists and vocalists of Hindustani and Carnatic music have been popular. And yet no one has yet surpassed Kanjeevaram Naina Pillai of yesteryears with his fantastic array of sidemen, providing the so-called "full-bench" concert fare with the violin, mridangam, kanjeeraa, dholak, ghatam, morsing and konnakol (vocalising of the drum syllables).

Though most of the composers in Carnatic music were born in the Thanjavur district, musicians in Andhra, Kerala and Karnataka were also responsible for keeping the flag of Carnatic music aloft.

Many princes in Andhra like Karvetinagar, Vijayanagar, Bobbili and Pithapuram patronised music. Parupalli Rama Krishnayya Pantulu, Veena Venkataswami Naidu were all names to conjure with.

In the Mysore court a great galaxy of musicians flourished such as Sadasiva Rao, Veena Seshanna, Bidaram Krishnappa, Vasudevachar, Muthiah Bhagavathar, Tigar Varadachariar and Chowdaiah.

In Thiruvananthapuram and Cochin many a musician was patronised. Noorani Parameswara Bhagavatar, Vadivelu, Coimbatore

Raghava Iyer, Palghat Anantharama Bhagavatar, Rama Bhagavatar, Veena Kalyanakrishna Bhagavatar, Chembai Vaidyanatha Bhagavatar, Palghat Mani Iyer, etc., did great service in propagating Carnatic music.

Though the music of the south is at least 2000 years old, the cutcheri paddhati has been established only in the last two centuries and we may name the pioneers of this format who were: Mahavaidyanatha Iyer, Patnam Subramani Iyer, Konerirajapuram Vaidyanatha Iyer, Ramnad Srinivasa Iyengar and Madurai Pushpavanam Iyer. Musicians who have contributed in no small measure to the formulation of the modern concert tradition are: Ariyakudi Ramanuja Iyengar, Maharajapuram Viswanatha Iyer, Chitoor Subramania Pillai, Flute Mali, Jalatarangam Subbaiyer, G.N. Balasubramaniam and Madurai Mani Iyer. Ariyakudi Ramanuja Iyengar deserves special mention for the planning, execution and balance of his cutcheries.

The term 'concert' is widely used to mean a 'cutcheri'. This is a misnomer. A concert means firstly, an agreement, or a union by mutual agreement; secondly, a musical entertainment, in which a harmonic combination of voices or sounds is effected. Our system of music based on melody cannot provide a 'concert' as it is known to western ears since harmonic arrangements of sounds are anathema to our system of music. Nor can we adopt the first meaning, as our concerts do not present a 'union by mutual agreement'. Sometimes there is neither union nor agreement among the performers. In such cases the concert becomes a 'dis' concerting experience for the listener.

We now come to the word 'cutcheri'. No one is able to pinpoint the date or place of its origin with certainty. It is believed to have been the adoption of the Urdu kach-hari, a court of law. *Pathak's Hindi Dictionary* lists a court of justice, as sizes, assembly, meeting and a public office under kach-hari. But by 1858 'cutcheri' came to mean not only an office, a court or a public place for business, but the ceremony of dancing at a wedding as recorded by C.P. Brown. It may be mentioned here that 'cutcheri' came to be associated with art performance only in South India. Scholars estimate that such an association gained currency in the last two or three hundred years.

Some decades ago the word 'vinigal' was used in the sense of cutcheri in Tamil papers and journals but has been completely superseded by cutcheri today. Other uses of the word in Tamil have associations with activities totally divorced from music such as Seettu Cutcheri (a session of card playing) and Arattai Cutcheri (a gossip session). But how and why the term came to mean a music performance is shrouded in mystery. There are those who argue that since music concerts were given mostly in courts in the past, the term kach-hari (court) became cutcheri to the layman.

3

VICISSITUDE IN VEENA TECHNIQUE

From the earliest times, the Veena has been the guiding star for the development of Indian Music in general. But Carnatic music cherished the 'Veena' and the yaazh as gifts of the gods and, through centuries of study and experiment, coaxed out of them a system of music that has no parallel in the whole world.

The human voice has a technique of training and execution adapted to the various systems of music. But Carnatic music enshrines its soil in gamakas. So its voice culture is a native of soil with its own distinct shade and colour.

Till about thirty years ago, the Veena was an aristocrat among instruments, professional Vainikas could be counted on one's fingers. Very few took to it as a pastime. It was a favourite with amateur lady singers whose fine voice blended with its delicate sound. It is not generally known that the Veena has an elaborate technique developed through centuries. It is so vast and subtle that a sound knowledge of the theory and practice of music has to be acquired before the Veena is taken up.

The South Indian (Saraswathi) Veena, in particular, mellows with the eye of its votary and unlocks, till this last moments, the esoteric secrets of sound that it treats in the depths of its soul. There is a faith corroborated by experience that this rarefied Veena music evolves continuously through repeated births till the dawn of cosmic consciousness.

The Veena with immovable frets has an advantage like the keys of a piano, the frets yield readily to the touch of a finger and alter notes that are sweet and vibrating with upper partials.

The advancement of modern Carnatic music is greatly indebted to the fixation of the twenty-four frets of the Veena. The present-day Veena with the fixed frets was an innovation of Govinda Dikshitar (17th century), father of Venkatamakhi. It is a well-known fact and oft-quoted maxim of our music veterans that the vocalist should learn the art of Veena playing if he/she were to acquire a fuller knowledge of the science of our music. This leads us to the importance of the proper fretting of the Veena.

In the fretting of the Veena, no hard and fast rule has been practised by the turners, excepting in the case of frets fixed by hearing the upper partials on the vibrating string. Most of the frets are fixed by the ear-test and trial and error method. If this ear-test should be the main method in the procedure of fretting, it would be ideal only if the turners were musicians of a high order. Even for musicians of high order, it requires a lot of concentration on their part to distinguish between a trishruti and a chatusshruti. The distinction between shrutis plays an important part in the process of Veena-fretting.

To enable the process of fretting the Veena to be done on scientific grounds, in proceeding from the known to the unknown and also to be sure the frequencies of notes obtained on the Veena, the following method is suggested.

The whole process of fretting the Veena is divided into three sections:

1. The fixing of eight of the frets by the method of overtones.
2. The fixing of seven mole to complete the first octave.
3. The remaining nine which are in the second set of twelve frets, to the octaves of those corresponding in the first set.

Main factors to be remembered—

1. The Veena should be provided with a new set of strings and tuned accurately in the panchama shruti.
2. The Veena should be tuned to the pitch at which it is likely to be played, tension being an important factor determining pitch.
3. The gradual slope of the wax should be examined so that the frets of higher frequency notes do not touch the vibrating

string when the frets of lower frequency notes are played.

4. The note with a lower frequency is preferred as with a slight deflection of the string, the higher frequency can be obtained.
5. The principle that the interval between two shrutis should not be less than a dvishruti should be observed.
6. After each step of procedure in Section 2, the Veena should be tuned back to panchama shruti accurately.
7. After fixing each note on the first or the second string their corresponding lower octaves on the third and the fourth strings should be tested.

The celebrities knew the left hand technique which is the key to genuine Veena music. The fore-finger and the middle-finger of the left hand have a purposeful function that tells them the different duties in the realm of musical phrase and diction.

First, the plucking or beat with the right hand fore-finger, middle-finger and the little-finger. The last moves upward and touches the three taalam (shruti) strings quite close upon each other, so that all chime together with no regular ding dong. The movement of the little-finger alternates with that of the thumb, so that there is a continuous drone like that of the Tambura. The Veena is the only instrument that sounds shruti and laya together. If the taalam strings are made of sound one after another at frequent intervals, it adds to the liveliness and tonefulness of music. Raagam and taanam need a subdued drone, care being taken to keep the beats quite irregular, as otherwise, they will wound like taalam. A balance between the sound of these strings and that of the playing ones is effected through choice of the correct gauge.

The movement of the plucking fingers is downward. It is an inexorable rule that they descend upon the strings alternately, and that the fore-finger and the little-finger act together and relieve the middle finger from all attention in Taalam. In solfa passages every note taken a beat, it is known as swara meettu. The other, saahitya meettu, covers more than one note. It generally goes by the letter in the saahitya. This rule is waived when there is need for examples or soft play. Another variety in plucking is Oli or kalvai meettu and tadai or Tattu meettu. The former keeps the sound of successive beats continuous, while the latter renders them staccato—one finger stops the sound produced by its companion. This device punctuates the sound produced monotony. Other varieties of meettu fall in the category of gamakas. The use of plectrums or artificial finger nails for the plucking fingers renders the sound sharp and continuous. The contact of a metal plectrum with a steel string produces a screech. It can be avoided with a little care, the correct shruti adjustment and can be tested by plucking all the four playing strings and all the three side strings together. But doing this often in the midst of playing for the sake of spectacular effect mars the even flow of melody and develops into a mannerism in course of time. There is nothing more relating to the right hand technique in genuine Veena play.

Of the two left hand fingers, the middle one has a very important role. The other is but an auxillary. The two fingers act together only in two contingencies, *viz.*, in swara meettu and kampita gamaka and its varieties such as Odukkal, Vali and Andolana. As mentioned earlier, plucking the strings and fingering the frets are complementary. Meettu and gamaka cannot be treated as separate items of technique. After all, music is an organic whole like the human body. Though vivisection, anatomy and physiology relate to the body, their objectives are different.

One of the chief functions of the middle-finger is to reduce plucking to the minimum. This is the essence of the traditional technique. A great deal of the charm of Veena music centres on the role of this finger. Here is a practical illustration of the first step in its function. This is the first casualty to the chaos that chokes Veena play and makes it a travesty these days. Hence the foremost need is for this attention.

Take the notes of Malavagowla, SR, GM, PD, NS are four pairs of ascending notes. Keep the length of the notes steady. Proceed at two notes for a beat. Start with the right hand fore-finger and the taalam of the little-finger. Play SR on the second string, Mandra Panchama—the left hand fore-finger for S and the middle-finger for R. Both S and R are played with one plucking with the right hand fore-finger. If the middle-finger descends with a gentle thud on the sixth fret of the second string, the sound produced is —R. Practise SR in this way till the taalam and notes coalesce and the sound is pleasant.

The playing fingers move in the same manner on the first string—the fore-finger for G, P and N and the middle-finger for M, D and S. Taalam falls on alternate pair—SR and PD. The playing fore-finger should always move on the string in both the ascent and descent. Only the other is raised a couple of inches high, so that it may gather a little force and perch on the specific frets with intensity. Practise the four ascending pairs—four plucking and two taalams for the octave.

The Avarohana or descent needs greater care and attention. The two playing fingers are on N and S when the Arohana or ascent is completed. Keep them as they are and sound one more S with the plucking finger and taalam. Before the sound dies down, take away the middle-finger for S with a gentle pull, so that the resulting N is clear and vibrant. Just as the playing middle-finger descends on the fret with a little force, it should likewise leave go of the string with a slight pull. The tow functions of the playing middle-finger are among the most vital aspects of traditional fingering. As mentioned earlier, the entire technique centres on this feature. The notes are plain, with no Gamaka. The emphasis lies on co-ordinating fingering and plucking with taalam going with the playing fore-finger.

The next step takes four notes for one beat. S starts on the first string and not on the second as before. Both the playing fingers always descend together on a string for the opening note. This is to ensure intensity of sound. This second step involves only one turn in the ascent and one in the descent for each of the plucking fingers and only one taalam for ascent and one for descent. The third step covers the whole octave in one plucking, up or down. This is a very salutary excercise in order to minimise plucking and yet keep the sound clear and crisp.

Trying these three steps on a few other scales like shankaraabharana, Todi, Kharaharapriya, Kalyaani and Pantuvaraali (Kaamavardhani) in different tempos will facilitate quick movement of the playing fingers, easy identification of frets for particular raagas, acquisition of steady rhythm, correct sense of swaraprasthaanas, systematic alternation of the plucking fingers, automatic lengthening of sound without the need for frequent plucking, keen perception of shruti, shuddha, etc.

A rational scientific method suited to the times is outlived. What is known as the Janta Swara or Aahatapratyaahata is a series of four important steps for practice. It involves interesting, impressive facets of Veena play, with a sparkling panorama of sound pictures emerging out of an intricate network of fingering.

Step No. 1(a)

Ascent (Aahata) : As usual, plucking fingers take a note per beat alternately. Every note repeats twice, making a total of sixteen ascending notes with four taalams. Take SS RR on the fifth and sixth frets of the second string (Mandra Panchama). Place the playing middle-finger on S and the fore-finger on the preceding fret. This is a uniform rule for Aahata. It is a point of interest that the twin notes are plucked by the right hand fore-finger and the middle-finger in turn, while the playing fingers reverse the order, the fore-finger bringing up the rear and leaving the principal role to its companion.

As the process goes up the octave, the first of the twin notes is simple. The second of the twins comprises two sounds—that of the previous fret on which the fore-finger rests coming in as a speek of sound linking the first and the repeated note. The twins on the second string sound SNS, RSR. The intervening auxiliary note is an inconspicuous link. The twins sound continuous, with no break in between. That is the pivot round which the whole series of four steps revolves. Aahata and Pratyaahata are ubiquitous in Veena music of quality. They do not stop with the practice stage.

Step No. 1(b)

Pratyaahata or descent is a more exacting step. The ascent stops with S N S. The first step in descent repeats the same. The first N is simple, the two fore-fingers working together. The linking note is always the tonic, S, sandwiched between the twins. In the descent, again, the two fore-fingers do the first of the twins, and the other two the second. Note the vital difference as between ascent and descent. In the case of the former, the link is the previous note. In the case of the latter, it is always the Adhara Shadja. In the former, again, the middle-finger plays both the twin notes, with the fore-finger as an auxiliary. But in the latter the fore-finger of the right hand and that of the left hand work together and produce the first of the descending twins, leaving the second to the other pair of fingers, *viz*. the two middle ones. The ascent takes four taalams and the descent four.

Step No. 2

The rule for ascent and descent is the same as Step No. 1. But this step proceeds in five groups for the ascent and five for the descent. A group has four twins, *e.g.*, SS RR GG MM. It is followed by the next, *viz*. RR GG MM PP. The other three are built up in the same manner. The jump from one group to another involves one Pratyaahata, when, for instance, RR of the second group follows MM of the first, and so on. M to R is Pratyaahata. So RR of the second group is played by Pratyaahata. Leaving out the first group, the first twins of the four take Pratyaahata. In the descend, the first twins take Aahata and the rest Pratyaahata. A simple rule for this and the following steps is that it is Aahata for forward fingering (move to the right) and Pratyaahata for backward or downward (move to the left) fingering.

Step No. 3

The second step turns back after the fourth twins. This one does so after the third and takes the next previous one as the fourth *e.g.* SS RR GG RR. Then follow the first four twins the whole step builds up that way. It can be seen that the second step involves only the Pratyaahata, but that this one has two, *viz.*, RR SS. The rest of the step is on the same lines.

Step No. 4

This has two new elements. There are long and short notes in every one of the five groups up and five down. Every group takes four taalams, of which the second falls in the middle of the second long note *e.g.* SA S Ri GG SS RR GG MM. Sa is twice as long as S. Ri is twice as long as R. It is Nedil and Kuril in Tamil or Deergha and Hrasva in Sanskrit. The taalam falls on Sa, cuts into Ri, falls on Sa and ends on G—four taalams for a group. But for these two new factors, this step falls in line with the other three.

The maximum time needed for learning these steps on the Veena is about ten hours. Four more practice steps complete the technique of fingering, before Gamakas are taken up.

Step No. 5

Six groups up and six groups down the octave. SR Ga RG Ma GM Pa MP Da PD Ni DN Sa SN Da Nd Pa DP Ma PM Ga MG Ri GR Sa. Each group takes a plucking. Alternate fingering gives three taalams for ascent and three for descent, at two groups or eight units for one taalam. For the sake of variety, take the scale of Kharaharapriya. Start S with a beat and play R with the fore-finger and Ga with the middle-finger. For the next five groups use the fore-finger for the first note and the other for the second and third in each group. Descent reverses the order of the playing fingers. A beat begins the first note of each group. The middle-finger hands the next two notes to the fore-finger with a pull from the string to give the sound intensity. This has been mentioned earlier in the chapter *viz.*, Avarohana for saahitya meettu. Try this step in different tempos and raagas, too.

Step No. 6

Six groups, all Hrasva (Sarvalaghu), for ascent and six for descent. Shankaraabharana SRGR, RMMG GMPM MPDP DNSN—SNDN NDPD DPMP PMGM MGRG GRSR. Take away the middle finger with a pull after the third note in every group. The fourth note will be there. Descent involves a change. The middle-finger starts the top S and leaves go of the string with a pull. The fore-finger plays ND and the middle-finger completes the group by perching on N. The rest is on the same lines.

Step No. 7

Harikaamboji. Eight phrases in the ascent and seven in the descent. RSSa GRRi Mgga PMMa DPPa NDDa SNNi RSSa. Delete the eight for the descent. Fore-finger plays RS. Middle-finger strikes the S fret on the second string with enough force so as to produce the note with no plucking. Play G with the middle-finger. Keeping the fore-finger on R. Take away the middle-finger with a pull. It is GR now, to be followed by Pratyaahata Ri with the middle-finger striking R. It is GRRi, a four unit phrase sounded by the right hand middle-finger. Fingering is the same for all the fifteen phrases.

Step No. 8

Keeravaani. The same number as 3. But the unit content of a phrase is eight, involving two pluckings for each phrase—four taalams for the ascent and four for the descent. This step combines 2 and 3 and the fingering becomes complicated in the process. The left hand middle-finger needs careful attention as it plays a major role in this step. When the step settles down to some order and discipline, a whole phrase has to be taken in one plucking. First stage : SRGR + RSSa RGMa + RRRi *etc.* till SRGR + RSSa of the higher octave. Second stage : SRGR RSSa RGMG GRRi etc.

Gamaka has been defined and its varieties mentioned in previous pages. The Raghunaatha Veena has been the most popular during the last three centuries. Subbaraya Sastri, son of Syama Sastri and Baluswami Dikshitar, brother of Mathuswami Dikshitar, are the earliest veterans whose Veena music has trickled down through generations to the present day.

Gamakas are unlimited in variety. The more of these subtle graces, the higher is the quality of music. But they have been given different names by different authors at different times.

A sensitive ear and sensitive fingers can evolve more interesting bits of fingering technique. This technique, gives unlimited scope for embellishing raaga, taana, Krithi, *etc.* That it has never enjoyed wide currency and yet it has managed to survive for generations is a baffling mystery. Taana is a very old word that originally meant a musical phrase. But somewhere in the last century it acquired a new connotation. The Naadaswaram was an open air instrument and specialised in raagam and pallavi. An elaborate raagam played for long hours was a common feature. The Tavil and the bronze cymbals maintained an even tempo of rhythm throughout to add zest to the recital and provide a sort of carpet for its smooth progress. Rakti was a device to present snatches of raagam in quick tempo and set the stage ready for the pallavi. It was also known as 'Madhyama Kaala Raaga Prastaara'.

The Veena took it over and adapted it to suit its own genius. The taalam strings, the technique of fingering and plucking and the wealth of gamaka came in quite handy for the development of a new feature of Veena music that scaled undreamt of heights of aesthetic beauty. It was so attractive that ere long the vocalist picked it up. Appropriately enough, he labelled it taanam and used the word as its sole text. When repeated over and over it changed into Ananta, infinity, signifying the interminable vista of scintillating sound images that flowed from it. By and by, the voice was assiduously cultivated to present all the nuances of the Veena.

That is the origin of the two styles of singing ghana, deep and reverberating and Naya, soft and melliferous, according to the structure of the voice and the direction given to it. There were experts who specialised in varieties of taana such as 'Maanava Taana', Mayura Taana, Markata Taana, Chakra Taana, Gajadhoti, Ashwadheti, Mandookarava, Jigibigi, Kukkuta Bhairavam etc. The last exponent of genuine taanam on traditional lines of voice culture passed away in 1927. What passes for taana today, both in voice and Veena, is a cheap tawdry mumbo-jumbo bereft of any music. In tune with the other aspects of Veena music taana, too, is, almost a lost art.

Among the string instruments, Veena is the only instrument which can not only produce 10 gamakas but also evoke certain grace notes. Playing upon two or three strings at the same time—a significant feature of the instrument—creates a beautiful effect as two octaves are sounded simultaneously which cannot be attempted in any other instrument not the human voice.

The different types of plucking method impart a unique

individuality to the instrument by which one can alternatively strike, pluck, twang, strum and glide over the strings. Thus the saahitya syllables can be better indicated on the Veena than any other instrument by which the emotive overtones and undertones find clear expression.

A. Veena Meettus

Different kinds of plucking or meettu are used in Veena playing. As mentioned in ancient musical works, these are:

(1) Tarjani meettu
Plucking the strings with the right hand index finger.

(2) Madhyama meettu
Plucking the strings with the right hand middle-finger.

(3) Kanishika meettu or laya meettu or pakka meettu
Plucking the taala strings with the right hand little-finger upwardly.

(4) Low meettu or keezh meettu and ul meettu
Striking the strings downwardly with the right hand fore-finger.

(5) Vali meettu or mel meettu
Striking the strings upwardly with the right hand fore-finger.

(6) Periya meettu
Plucking the strings forcefully.

(7) Sanna meettu
Plucking the strings softly.

(8) Gotu meettu
Low meettu and laya meettu done simultaneously.

(9) Pattu meettu
Plucking the string with the right hand index-finger, and stopping it immediately with the right hand middle-finger.

(10) Vidpu meettu
Letting the strings free after the pattu meettu.

(11) Kodi meettu

Placing the finger lightly on the first playing string and then lifting it.

(12) Kuttu meettu

Plucking all the four playing strings with the right hand index, middle and ring-fingers simultaneously.

(13) Vidi meettu

Plucking the third, second and first strings one by one.

(14) Kathiri meettu

Plucking with the right hand index-finger and middle-finger sharply one after the other so as to produce a tremulous effect.

(15) Svara meettu

Plucking the strings for all the swaras.

(16) Saahitya meettu

Plucking the strings for saahitya letters alone.

B. The Technique of Plucking

Sarngadeva in the Vaadya Adhyaaya of *Sangita Ratnakara* while discussing on the various aspects of Veena and its other functions specifically devotes a section for the plucking or striking technique of the instrument. It is as follows:

(1) Ghata :

Pluck the string with fore-finger and stop the sound with the middle.

(2) Pata :

A simple stroke or a beat.

(3) Samlekha :

A descending formation upon a phace or a long note.

(4) Ullekha :

Quick succession of two beats repeating the same note, first with the fore-finger and the second with the middle-finger.

(5) Analekha :

Stopping with the thumb, the sound produced by the middle-finger.

(6) Bhramara :

Pressing four fingers for a rapid succession of sound.

(7) Sandhitha :

Playing the Ghata method with the help of middle and ring fingers.

(8) Chinna :

Plucking with the fore-finger and ring-finger in quick succession.

(9) Nakha Karthari :

A rapid volley of notes played with four finger nails.

Sarngadeva also speaks of plucking with the left hand with a couple of finger touches known as Shphurita and Khasita. Besides these eleven thirteen more pluckings are evolved by Sarngadeva which are executed jointly by the fingers of both the hands.

1. Ghosha, 2. Repha, 3. Bindu, 4. Karthari, 5. Arthakarthari, 6. Nishkotita, 7. Skhalita, 8. Suka vakthra, 9. Murchana , 10. Talahasta, 11. Ardhachandra, 12. Prasara and, 13. Kahara.

During his time the right hand fingers played a predominent part. This tradition continues even now in Hindustani music and it is reverse in Carnatic music. The tradition referred to here centres on the separate role of two left hand fingers. The right hand fingers pluck the strings alternately and the little finger for the rhythm. The rhythmic strings are the pakka sarani have the role of rhythm and shruti.

4

TRADITION AND STYLES OF VEENA PLAYING

The Saraswati Veena of South India is, today, one of the foremost concert instruments. As contrasted with its gradual eclipse in the North by the Sitar and Sarod, the Veena in the South has risen to greater heights than ever before in popularity, even as the technique of playing it has advanced.

To the lay listener, all Veena recitals may look alike, but the discerning ear can distinguish different styles of Veena playing. The technique of Veena playing today can be broadly divided into three basic schools: the Thanjavur, Andhra and Mysore Schools. Each school has a proud heritage of its own, and there are purists even today who zealously guard their precious traditions. However, it is easily noticeable that due to constant exposure of each school to the others through the radio and other modern media, there has been a merging of styles to some extent.

1. The Thanjavur School

Players of the Thanjavur School aim at reproducing the vocal style as closely as possible. This approach has been developed right from the heyday of the Thanjavur court and has been moulded and polished to perfection in this direction. No effort is spared to imitate vocal music.

Vidwan K.S. Narayanaswamy, one of the eminent Veena exponents belonging to this school, says that uccharippu is of utmost importance—the pronunciation and accent on each syllable of the saahitya is to be transferred to the Veena exactly as it is sung. The raaga aalaapana, taanam, rendering of the Krithi, as well as niraval and swaras are in this mould. Raaga aalaapana is elaborate and replete with deep gamakas or graces. The pace is maintained leisurely. Fast passages are eschewed, for fear that gamakas and finger nuances will be lost. Such types of meettu or plucking, as kathiri meettu and tribhinna are avoided. It is a stately and dignified style whose classical appeal can never fade.

The traditional Thanjavur School gave rise to three distinct styles of Veena technique. K.S. Narayanaswamy belongs to the vocal or gayaki style described above.

The late Karaikudi Brothers—Subbarama Iyer (who played the Veena holding it vertically) and Sambasiva Iyer—developed this style further in their own individualistic manner. They were famous for their elaborate raaga aalaapana and taanam—they painted the raaga picture on a large, wide canvas, so to speak, and their imagination seemed endless.

Delineation of a single raaga could go on for hours. One distinct peculiarity about this style is the handling of the Saadhaarana gaandhaara in the raaga Todi. Usually the gaandhaara or ga is played on the chatushruti rishabha fret with a deep gamaka (except in the panchama varjotha pharases such as ga-ma-dha-ni-sa where, occasionally, gamaka is avoided). However, in the Karaikudi style, it is played on its own fret without any gamaka throughout, except occasionally where gamaka is used. This 'flat' playing of 'ga' lends a completely different colour to the raaga—a slight Hindustani touch at this point—and this feature instantly identifies the Karaikudi style.

Veena Dhanammal was also of the Thanjavur School, but developed the art in her own unmistakable way to such an extent that she was totally individualistic and in a class of her own. Her style was deceptively simple and pleasing to the ear. In an effort to reproduce the vocal gamaka, she employed an elaborate left hand technique — separation of the fingers, the occasional use of a gentle pluck with the left hand finger, and various other devices. This produced an effort similar to the sweet tinkling of silver bells. The fact that her Veena was tuned to a higher pitch (equivalent to the female voice, about G or G – shape enhanced this effect.

Her raaga aalaapanas and taanams were short and concise. Yet it seemed as if nothing more remained to be said, and the essence of the raaga was extracted and presented. Krithis were performed in a rounded, complete manner. Niraval was used, but Kalpana swaras were scrupulously avoided. Her specialities were padams and jaavalis. She would improvise and elaborate each line of a padam (breaking into song now and then) with so many fine nuances at every turn of the phrase that it could never be exactly reproduced again by anyone. She was a living legend in her time, but unfortunately there are very few records where this style can be heard. Today there is no one who can be truly said to reflect her style fully.

These, then, are the three branches of Thanjavur (style) School.

A highly individualistic Vainika of modern times who tried to further improve upon the Thanjavur approach to Veena playing was S. Balachandar. He developed his own style which is characterised by the meena gamaka borrowed from the North Indian Sitar. He used it to play four or five notes on a single fret in an attempt to eliminate unnecessary plucking and thus bring it closer to the vocal style. He did employ fast passages as contrasted with the orthodox Thanjavur tradition, and his style can be described as virile and aggressive. Raaga aalaapana was his forte and he was able to uncover hidden beauties even in rare and vivaadi mela raagas.

2. The Mysore School

The Mysore School developed in quite a different direction. It has an equally hoary tradition of great Vainikas in Seshanna, Subbanna, Venkatagiriappa, and his disciple Mysore Doreswamy Iyengar. The latter describes the Mysore style as basically an instrumental style, in which the melodic parity of the notes is sought to be retained. Therefore, deep gamakas are not generally used. Shallow gamakas, playing the notes on the frets, a pleasing meettu, are of tribhinna (plucking the three strings simultaneously or successively) for a piano forte effect, use of jana swaras in phrases like Sa-ni-ni-dha dha-pa-pa-ma and dhaatu swaras such as ri-pa-ga-dha ma-ni-pa-sa are typical of this style. Left hand fingers are separated to facilitate fast passages. The raaga aalaapana is presented on these lines, and the taanam typical of Mysore is full of melodic effects achieved by the use 'chitta taana' (present taanam), says Doreswamy Iyengar. These were extensively used for practice to enable the student to gain speed and clarity. Many raagas such as Behag, Jhinjhoti and Khamaas played by Vainikas of the Mysore School have a distinct North Indian touch, due to the proximity of Karnataka's northern districts to Maharashtra and the ensuing influence. It is very pleasing and reposeful style.

3. The Andhra School

The Andhra School of Veena playing can be distinguished by the variety of meettus used, the elaborate right hand technique and a few high speed passages employed in rendering the raaga and the taanam. Veena Venkataraman Daas of Vizianagaram was famous for his shatkala or 6 speed taanam—with the Veena in vertical position. Sangameshwara Sastri was another well-known artiste of this style. It is said that they used to perform Veyisadhakam. That is practising the alankaaras in the three octaves in three speeds non-stop a thousand times every day. This they used to do for three months and it served them to go without any further practice during the rest of the year. Vasa Krishnamurthy is one of the Vidwans of this style.

Emani Sankara Sastri, although of this Andhra School (his father Achutharama Sastri was another Vainika who played the Veena holding it vertically), had merged the Thanjavur style and Andhra style and had further improved upon this merger. He used a wide range of gamakas and meettus to achieve an extraordinary variety of textures and modes in his music. He was perhaps the only Vainika to modulate the volume of the pluck to suit the music, from very soft to very loud, and the texture from a harsh staccato to a pluck so soft that it is startingly like a human voice. He used all the fingers of his right hand to produce these various effects and also for producing harmonic effects by using tribhinna and other gamakas. By modulating the pluck and employing the Thanjavur style he brings it closer to the human voice. At the same time, he maximses the potentiality of the instrument by producing purely string effects which are equally beautiful. Raaga aalaapana is traditional, yet alive with a new freshness. A raaga like Bhairavi is clothed in garments of new splendour by an unusual turn of the phrase of juxtaposition of notes; yet it does not lose its identity. Mandhra sthaayi elaboration is interspersed with madhya sthaayi phrases producing the effect of samvaadam or a duet concert. He freely uses folk idioms to enrich the aaalaapana. Taanam is replete with instrumental sound effects and is played in three speeds. The total impression conveyed by this style is a sense of completeness in all respects. Emami Sankara Sastri could perhaps be called the pioneer of the modern styles of Veena playing.

Most of the younger generation of Veena players do not rigidly adhere to any one style, but borrow and merge different styles freely. There are of course, areas where pure tradition is preserved even now, but these are rare. Every distinct style that emerges today is more individualistic than belonging to any particular school.

With the influence of folk music, North Indian Music, Western Classical Music and Jazz, techniques have improved and been perfected, new ideas are emerging, and perhaps the day is not far off when the traditional Veena will discover new frontiers in Carnatic Music.

5

LUMINARIES OF DIFFERENT STYLES

The Vainika tradition of Thanjavur may be said to have emerged since the period of King Raghunatha Naayak in the 17th century and it continued to have a glorious history for nearly three centuries till the beginning of the 20th century A.D.

The reference to the presence of Vainikas, musicians and composers in the court of Thanjavur is found in the pages of *Ṣahitya Ratnakara* and *Sangita Sudha*. King Raghunatha has described himself as an expert Vainika, with a remarkable degree of proficiency in playing aalaapana, thaya, gita, prabandha, for Nata Raaga. Taanas meant for being played and for practice in Veena were said to have been composed by Govinda Dikshitar, the guru and minister of the Naayak ruler. Further, the expounding of the pakkasarani maarga of taana playing in the pages of *Chaturdandi Prakasika*, by Venkatamakhi establishes the emergence of a recognisable Vainika sampradaaya as distinct from the gaayaka sampradaaya.

In the subsequent centuries, special illustrative taana prayogas intended for voice and instruments were composed for a number of raagas and these were referred to as gatra dandi and jantra dandi. The Maratha Rajas were themselves composers and musicians, no wonder they appointed vaaggeyakaras, Vainikas and musicians in their court. Fourtunately, it is these court musicians who had continued the Vainika tradition as prevalent in the court. We are able to collect some names of the Vainikas as some of them were well-known. Excepting a few cases, the biographical details of these Vainikas are lacking. The reference to their having been contemporaries of a particular patron-ruler, however, helps us to fix the period in which they lived.

Documentary evidence attesting to the existence of three notable families of Vainikas who adorned the Thanjavur court during the 18th and 19th centuries, is fortunately, available in the archives of the Saraswati Mahal Library. This information is valuable from the point of research relating to the chronology, biography and assessment of the contribution of composers and musicians of the court.

A detailed study of the technique may follow a notice of outstanding luminaries who were prominent in the early decades of this century. They were sincerely devoted to the art and achieved a measure of success through unremitting toil. Many of them never displayed their art to the galaxy or for mass appeal. The following short biographical details and their achievements are briefly discussed here. The personalities discussed belong to the different samsthaana or areas of South India. Some of them were:

Veena Kalahasti Ayya

A well-known Vainika vidwan who flourished in the court of Tulaja-II. He hailed from a family of musicians. It is from one record that we are able to get some biographical details of this Vainika. His father Veena Ramalingayya and his grand-father, Veena Vaidyapa were also Veena players. Tulaja had great regard for his musical attainments and honoured him. A record in the Modi script dated 1881 A.D. states that Tulaja presented him the village of Perannur and also one veli of nanjai land and one-fourth veli of punjai land to be wholly enjoyed by Kalahasti Ayya and his family and by his descendants after his demise. It is further stated that there was no necessity to renew the grant every year and the original grant document was handed over to the family of Kalahasti Ayya.

The geneology of the musician as found in the grant is useful from the point of view of research. Veena Ramalingayya was Kalahasti Ayya's father while his grand-father was well-known as Veena Vaidyappa. Both were masters of music and eminent players on the instrument.

The court of Tulaja was the exponents in vocal and instrumental music. Their documentary evidence which bear eloquent testimony to Tulaja's great love of fine arts and his munificence in spending lavishly towards the growth and welfare of the art and artists.

Of the aasthaana vidwans who adorned the Thanjavur courts during the time, Veena Kalahasti Ayya was well-known. He hailed from a family of musicians. It is from the written documents of 1771 A.D. in Modi script recording Tulaja's grant of sarvamaanya land to Veena Kalahasti Ayya that we are able to learn his geneology.

Tradition points out to a fact that one Veena Kalahasti Iyer, a Vainika, as Tyagaraja's maternal grand-father who was also the recipient of royal honour and patronage in the form of lands and house. But the gotra Kalahasti Ayya as indicated in the grant and that of Tyagaraja happens to be the same. Therefore, the former cannot be identified as Tyagaraja's maternal grand-father. In the history of our vaaggeyakaaras and musicians, we are confronted with identical names being given to grand parents and children in order to preserve the family identification. In such circumstances, it is difficult to identify the composers.

It is said that Veena Kalahasti Ayya had trained disciples such as (1) Veena Perumalayya, (2) Dipambapuram Kasturirangayya and (3) Sonti Venkataramanayya, guru of Tyagarajaswami.

Venkataramana Das of Vizianagara (1866-1948)

Seven generations of his ancestors were Vainikas. His Veena had a small sound-box and a narrow Danda; but its gourd was big. He held the Veena vertically. He practised for ten hours a day, using all the fingers except the thumbs. He was a master of speed. On account of the vertical posture the left hand fingers of music that flited like lightning. He set up a record for taanam in quick tempo. His was spectacular music displaying feats of prowess and jugglery of sound.

Ananda Gajapati, an enlightened ruler of Vizianagaram and a connoisseur of art, made him his court musician and gave him a seat by his side in recognition of his talents. He was held in such popular esteem that a street of Vizianagaram was named after him.

Pithapuram Sangameswara Sastri (1874-1931)

Like Venkataramana Das, Sastri held his Veena vertically. The Dandi was broad and afforded room for deflecting the strings. He specialised in producing a whole octave on a fret. So, his play had plenty of curves and sounded like Gotu Vaadyam and the North Indian Sarod. He was a naada Yogi and spend all his waking hours in practice. The superb, majestic volume and the effortless ease with which he worked wonders on the Veena spread his fame far and near. Gurudev Tagore invited him to Shantiniketan for a long stay with him.

The Maharajah of Pithapuram was Sastri's patron. Both Das and Sastri paid greater attention to the right hand technique than to the left. The one shone by speed and the other by curve. Microtones based on the 22 shruti basis and subtle gamakas did not receive attention to their hands. Manipulation of sound was their forte. Their raagam, taanam and pallavi were the fruits of hard work. Their music was profound and magnificent, though not inspired. As both of them belonged to Andhra Pradesh, traces of their Veena music still linger in a few hands in the region.

Mysore Seshanna (1852-1926)

It is given only to a fortunate few that their fame lasts long after their passing away. Seshanna is inordinately lucky in this respect. His career was glamorous, if not spectacular, favoured by fortune, rather than by the mass. Muthiah Bhagavathar was equally glamorous, but he left no trail behind, as Seshanna has done.

The Maharajah of Mysore was very fond of Seshanna. He used his standing and influence to keep his favourite on the crest of the waves. Seshanna was invited to Baroda, where he was seated in a silver palanquin and taken round in a procession, many are the legend that recount his glory.

His music was flowed like sweet honey. Seshanna did not believe in depth or intensity. He played on the Veena and with it . A few light, staccatto touches with gimmicks on the four strings with the right hand fingers did the job. Seshanna's regal mein and the joy he diffused all around him by his own ecstasy was nothing if not contagious. A few strokes of Hindustani diction established his virtuosity in both the styles. His taanam was often indistinguishable from raagam. His nimble fingers flew up and down the octave weaving figures of threes and fours like a dummy horse drum and came to a stop with a bang, striking the four strings together. This element of his style persists even today among Vainikas of Mysore. It is a sound manipulation that is neither raagam, nor taanam nor swaram, but a cheap clap trap that is titillating though not edifying.

He also learnt music with his father Chikkaramappa and later with Mysore Sadasiva Rao. On his style a great deal can be said about his meettu which was so nature and rich that he could elaborate a raaga for more than an hour without repeating. His sense of taala was such that he could improvise hundreds of aavartha without loosing its artistic beauty. He has composed several varnam, swarajathi, tillaana, Krithi, *etc.*

Among his disciples Veena Venkatagiriappa, Srirangam Ramaswamy Iyengar are famous Vainikas.

Bakshi Subbanna (1855-1938)

A contemporary of Seshanna and colleague in the Durbar gallery of musicians, he was a more substantial and serious-minded exponent of the Veena. But he was an introvert and lacking in push and enterprise. In spite of Seshanna's popularity and country wide fame, Subbanna enjoyed the respect and esteem of the better informed among patrons of music.

Sonti Venkataramanayya

He was the illustrious son of Sonti Venkatasubbayya who was a junior contemporary of Adiyappaya and the composer of the beautiful varna in Bilahari raaga in praise of Tulaja and a taana varna in Purvikalyaani 'Ninnukori'. Sonti Venkataramanayya lived during the reign of Tulaja and Sarabhoji and was the most favourite among the court vidwans. He enjoyed the unique privilege of sharing the 'ardhasimhaasana' with King Tulaja and delighting the audience on every new Year's day by his excellent performance.

Venkataramanayya was honoured with the titles of 'Taana Vidyayama Sadrisa' and 'Gaayaka Saardula' which reveal his skill in playing taana and his proficiency in Veena and singing.

Mahipalai Veena Perumalayya

He hailed from a family of Vainikas who were Andhra Brahmins. Having learnt Veena from Veena Kalahasti Ayya, he became an expert in handling ghana raaga taana. It is said that he played Bhairavi in an elaborate manner without repetition, in appreciation of which Sarbhoji presented him with a village known as Mahipalai. He was also honoured by Raghunatha Tondaiman of Pudukottai. According to Sri Subbarama Dikshitar, Veena Perumalayya was a good Vainika and also a fine composer. To him are ascribed the two varnas, one in Sourashtra and another in Saaveri, which are, however, not traceable. Of his two brothers, Veena Narayanaswamy was a fine performer, while Kodandaiya, was a composer of Svarajatis.

Paccimiriyam Adiyappayya

The famous composer of the immortal 'viriboni' varna in Bhairavi, was by Adiyappayya who adorned the court of Pratapasimha and Tulaja II (1787-1798). He was an exponent of the Veena and Sri Subbarama Dikshitar refers to him as "Taana Varna Maargadarsi". The varna presents the essence of the raaga through the artistic employment of all the characteristic prayogas occurring in the raga. His son Veena Krishna Ayya was also an eminent Vainika and the composer of the 'Sapta Talesvara Prabandha'.

Veena Subbiah and Veena Subbukutti Ayya

Also belonged to the line of Adiyappayya. Reference points out to Veena Tirumalai Ayya and Veena Annachi Iyer as contemporary court vidwans during the period of Sarabhoji-II.

Pallavi Gopalayya, the composer of the famous ata taala varnas in Todi and Kalyani Raagas *viz.* 'Kanakangi' and 'Vanajakshi' was also an expert Vainika and was court vidwan during Sarabhoji's reign (1798-1843).

Of the Thanjavur Quartette, Sivanandam was a Vainika and a composer. All the four brothers adorned the Thanjavur court for some time. The ancestors of Veena Dhanammal (1867-1938) were eminent vidushis of the Thanjavur court.

Dharmayya Ramasamayya

He was a court Veena vidwan during the period of Sarabhoji and was one of the famous musicians of the time. A profound scholar in Telugu, Sangita and Sahitya. In addition to his eminence in Veena playing, he carried the portfolio of Superintendent of Msicians in the court of Thanjavur. We find records in which his name occurs as the Chief Superintendemt of Music and Naataka Saala Department. He attended to the supervision of the repair of musical instruments, purchase of strings and issue of orders in respect of remuneration to musicians.

Chikka Line of Vainikas

Chikka Othappayya Garu was the famous Vainika of Thanjavur and his family had the reputation of being the custodians of dharma and charity. His line produced eminent Vainikas of the age such as (1) Veena Dharmayya, (2) Tsallagali Viraraghavayya, (3) Tsallagali Gopalayya, (4) Dasavadyam Krishnayya, (5) Ramaswamayya, (6) Veena Adimurthy, (7) Appayya, (8) Mysore Veena Subayya, (9) Varahappa Dikshit, (10) Veena Atmaramayya and (11) Fiddle Venkataramayya.

Varahappayya

The illustrious son of Dharmayya was a private minister to Sivaji-II. He learnt Veena from his father. He could play Western music on the Piano. He mastered the English language and performed on the Violin before an English audience at Madras which elicited the admiration of the British. He was the Superintendent of the villages during the reign of Sarbhoji-II and Commander-in-Chief of the native regiment of the Thanjavur Samasthaanam. He also held the coveted post of Superintending the musicians of the palace, including Hindustani, Western and Carnatic musicians. Many music manuscripts were copied and transcribed under the orders of Varahappayya, as evidenced by the fly leaves of these manuscripts. State documents in the Modi script record these details (140-c 1886-3-TMSSM Library). It is said that he prepared a detailed catalogue and index of the several manuscripts in the library. Among the disciples who learnt Veena and Violin from him may be mentioned Parameswara Bhagavatar, Lakshmana Gosayee and Paramesvara Gosayee. His son Sri Ramayya Dikshit learnt Veena and Piano from his father.

Veena Appayya

Brother of minister Varahappayya. He mastered Western and Indian musical instruments. He was exceptionally good in Hindustani music and was honoured by many Samasthaanas. He was a Veena vidwan in the Thanjavur Samasthaanam.

Tsallagali Viraraghavayya

Brother of Vijayavarahappa was alias Veena Dharmayya. He adorned the Thanjavur Samasthaanam as a prominent Vainika. He used to sing and produce such melodious music on his Veena, that he was awarded the title "Tsallagali" (cool southern breeze) by the Samasthaanam. His son Tsallagali Gopalayya also adorned the court.

Tsllagali Krishnayya (1822-1866)

Another expert Vainika of the court, who was called "Abhinava Narada". On account of the sweet melody of his Veena, he was called Tsallagali Krishnayya. His disciples were (1) Tiruvalangadu Tyagaraja Dikshitar, (2) Velu Kanchi Sadasivayyagaru, (3) Kanchi Nilakantha Sastri (4) Mayavaram Vaidyanatha Iyer and (5) Akhilandapuram Dikshitar.

Mysore Veena Sambayya

Another descendent of the illustrious Chikka line was Veena Sambayya. He went over to Mysore Samasthaanam where he became the court vidwan. His Veena playing was noted for its rich volume. Tillaanas were said to be the highlights of renderings, with an attractive plucking technique. His son was Veena Bangaruswamy Ayya, who also became Mysore Samasthaana vidwan. It is said that the famous Chikkaramappa, the reputed Vainika of the Mysore court and the father of the great Veena Seshanna belonged to the Chikka line of Vainikas.

Veena Atmaramayya and Fiddle Venkatachalam Ayya

Were the nephews of Varahappa Dikshitar and they adorned the Thanjavur court. Later they went to Pudukottah where they became very famous. Fiddle Venkatachalam Ayya's son *viz.* Veena Ramaswamy Ayya and Veena Lakshmanaswamy Ayya were also musicians.

Veena Adimurthy Ayya

A cousin of Tsallagali Krishnayya, was one of the leading aasthana vidwans and his son Veena Venkatachalam Ayya, was an expert musician.

6

FOUR SCHOOLS OF TRADITION AND STYLE

This chapter is a follow-up study on the schools or bani that followed the tradition of those personalities (discussed in Chapter 5) who incessantly tried and succeeded in achieving merited attention in the realm of Carnatic music. In this Chapter I have tried to identify and distinguish three basic styles in Veena whose representatives are at present not with us. They are :

Karaikudi Sambasiva Iyer and Subbarama Iyer (KARAIKUDI SCHOOL)

Veena Dhanammal (DHANAM SCHOOL)

Emani Sankara Sastri (ANDHRA SCHOOL)

Devakottai Narayana Iyengar (KARAIKUDI SCHOOL)

The Karaikudi Veena Brothers

Through the years, the art of Veena playing has produced many great musicians. Among these, in the Carnatic music world, the Karaikudi Brothers stand out, towering above most others, for their mastery of the art, which was the result of complete dedication and incessant practice, their abiding faith in tradition and their virtual rejection of all other material things not connected with their music. It is they who created, within the framework of the highly regarded Thanjavur tradition or style, what is known today as the Karaikudi paani.

For the Karaikudi Brothers, Subbarama Iyer (1883-1936) and

Sambasiva Iyer (1888-1958), to be Vainikas. One encounters a series of Vainikas of note : Malayappa Iyer (c. 1750) who was himself to the third generation of this Vainika family, Venkateswara Iyer (c. 1780), Subbaraya Iyer (c. 1810) and Subbayya also known as Subbarama Iyer (c. 1840). The last named was the court musician of Pudukottai and the father of the Brothers.

The late S.Y. Krishnaswami, a connoisseur, once wrote that there are three influences that combine to create a genius in art: the first is the inherent flair and ability; the second, heredity; and the third, unremitting practice. Repetition is like dhyaanam, meditation. In meditation, one repeats the same mantra again and again and does not go in for a new mantra every day. So also, perfect music is possible only by it being practised again and again. It was the understanding and the application of this secret that clothed the inherent talent.

According to the Karaikudi Brothers, these have to be practiced initially for three to five years and, even after acquiring mastery over all aspects of music, these basic exercises have to be part of the practice sessions of musicians throughout their lives.

The Brothers played as one but had their own distinctive ways of handling the instrument. The elder Subbaramma Iyer held the Veena in a vertical position, the only prominent Vainika to do so in Tamil Nadu. Sangameswara Sastri and Venkataramana Das, Veena vidwans of Bobbili and Vizianagaram in Andhra, also adopted this 'urdhva' style of holding the Veena considering it the manly way of doing it. So too did Emani Achyutarama Sastri, father of Emani Sankara Sastri. But Sambasiva Iyer held his Veena in the horizontal position, the one which is common today.

Holding the Veena vertically seems to have been the ancient practice, blessed by sastraic sanction. This is the way the Veena is depicted in ancient sculptures and paintings. The musical concert format now prevailing is less than 150 years old and the Veena, to start with, was the accompanying instrument for vocalists and continued to be so till it was supplanted by the violin. It would seem that the practice of holding the Veena vertically while accompanying a vocalist was found to be inconvenient and was gradually replaced by the horizontal style.

When they played, they were lost in their music and often were not even aware of what was happening. Tirugokarnam Krishnamurthy Iyer, a nephew of Subbarama Iyer, recalls an interesting anecdote which illustrates this aspect. Krishnamurthy Iyer was then a student in the Sangeetha Bhushanam course in the Annamalai University. A concert of the Karaikudi Brothers, with Pudukottai Dakshinamurthy Pillai providing the mridangam support, took place in the campus.

As the Brothers played the Krithi 'Ambanadu Vinnapamu' in Todi raaga and embarked on a niraval, Pillai was playing at his best, but all the time with the feeling that it was not good enough. They followed a great exhibition of Kalpanaaswaras. At one moment, it appeared as if the exercise was ending, but the Brothers switched over to a different swara pattern and started soaring again. This went on repeatedly, making Dakshinamurthy Pillai marvel at the masters' musicianship. Finally, the song came to a close, to the thunderous applause of the large audience. Later, in the privacy of their lodgings, Dakshinamurthy Pillai asked Subbarama Iyer "Aandavane, why this extraordinary outburst? Should you not have had some mercy on a poor man like me?" Iyer replied, "Why, I did nothing extraordinary, I played only as usual."

Subbarama Iyer received his musical training from his father Subbayya Iyer. Karaikudi was, as it were, the capital of Chettinad, the land of Nattukottai Chettiars. Apart from the Karaikudi Brothers, some other famous musicians were at that time resident in Karaikudi—like Mazhavarayanendal Subbarama Bhagavatar (who was awarded the title of Sangeetha Kalaanidhi by the Music Academy, Madras in 1942). Rajamani Iyenger (guru of famous cine playback singer, T.M. Soundararajan) and Karaikudi Srinivasa Iyengar (whose son was married to the daughter of Ramanuja Iyengar) who belonged to Ariyakudi, a nearby village.

Subbarama Iyer was passing through a financially difficult time. Dispirited as he was, when an astrologer friend did his bit by telling him that there was a danger to his life a few months hence, he felt convinced that the mission in his life was coming to an end. The day prior to his demise, in 1936, Subbarama Iyer asked his relatives to retire for the day early, as they would have a lot of work to do the next day.

Sambasiva Iyer was generally quite reluctant for taking on any student. When Samathu Iyengar, grand-father of Devakottai Narayana Iyengar, went to him seeking his services as guru for his grandson, he demanded a fee of 2000 rupees, to put him off. Some time later he did take on Narayana Iyengar as a disciple, at his brother's behest, but the guru-sishya relationship lasted only 3 years.

For long, Iyer had been experimenting with different strings for the Veena to achieve an improved tone. He had discovered that winding silver or copper wire of specified gauge around the mandra and anumandra strings improved their tone. He has also devised a hand-operated machine, made out of bicyle parts, with which to do the winding properly. Now the combined insights and skills of Iyer and Ramanathan led to the development of a proto type on an electrically operated wire-winder and to the improvement of the final products. The strings thus produced became known as Sambasiva Iyer strings.

Sambasiva Iyer was a man of few words. His conversations were always brief. His whole life was dedicated to the pure exposition of the Veena to produce music in the grandest and most authentic manner.

Features of the Karaikudi Bani

Every style of music has its devotees as well as its detractors. The Karaikudi Bani of Veena playing is no exception; it too has been the subject of partisan pronouncements.

A discriminating listener should, however, note of distinctive features of each style—and understand the style in its proper perspective—in order to avoid his or her likes and dislikes being mere prejudices.

The Karaikudi Bani of Veena playing, made familiar within living memory by the Karaikudi Brothers, is part of the broader Thanjavur tradition to which Veena Dhanammal at one end, and a modern-day master like S. Balachandar at the other, both belong. It falls in between.

Dhanammal was part of a music tradition which found expression mainly in singing. She too could not sing and, if she was a family exception as a Vainika, her handling of the instrument yet emphasised the vocal or gayaki approach. In her playing, the emphasis was almost exclusively on the melodic content. Her performance was more suggestive than explicit and in that respect more poetic. She avoided complex instrumental techniques to give expression to her inner musical realisations. She produced the gamakas or graces rather more by executing slides on the stem of the Veena than by the pulling or lateral deflection of the strings to produce oscillations.

The technique of the Karaikudi Brothers emphasised gamaka by deflection but not to the extent done by Balachandar.

Their gamakas, devoid of exaggeration and by no means simple oscillations, were characterised by a degree of sharpness and yet intimated beautiful nuances, artistic, curves. In their hands, the playing of gamaka was a case of technique translated into art and art concealing art.

Another contrast, Dhanammal's music was essentially lakshya-oriented. That of the Karaikudi Brothers paid equal attention to the lakshana aspects.

(The comparisons are made to highlight the distinctiveness of each style, not to denigrate the one or the other).

The Bani as given expression to by the Brothers is characterised by certain other important features. These are :

The use of the shoping technique employing the hand.

The absence of vibrato, the simple vibratory oscillation on a fret, including the 'sa' and 'pa' frets.

The avoidance of the 'kartari' meettu, which is a right hand pluck employed to produce compound sounds like 'krr' and 'tru'.

The use of taala strings for the purpose of keeping taala while playing compositions.

The stumming of the main strings for effect and as an expression of inwardly felt pulsations.

The rare use of tribhinna (or of playing of triple notes) principally, to aid the interpretation of saahitya (*e.g.* while rendering the same-note phrase 'Paramasambhava' in the Kaapi Narayani composition Sarasa Saama-dhana.

The use of a special technique to produce 'ravai' sangatis or fast variations.

The use of jantas (notes in pairs) in taanam rendering.

The use of plectra for plucking.

In the heydays of the Brothers, there was no artificial amplification of sound at concerts. So, they worked on and perfected a method of producing volume without sacrificing sensitivity.

It is said that 500 persons gathered on a float during the annual teppam or float festival in Karaikudi could clearly hear the Brothers play. The Brothers would have frowned on the use of the contact mike, for the resulting loss of sensitivity would have been unacceptable to them.

The Brothers played as one, but those who have listened to them noted a difference in emphasis but without difference in style.

Veena Dhanammal

Her heritage was the Thanjavur tradition in music and dance, a tradition enriched and exemplified by the devadasi community to which she belonged. The family records go back to Papammal, her grandmother's grandmother who was a musician-dancer in the Thanjavur court a couple of hundred years ago, in the 18th century. Her grandmother Kamakshi, a court-dancer who had learnt Sadir from Bharatam Ganapathi Sastri, uncle of Patnam Subramaniya Iyer, was reputedly an excellent singer as well. She learnt music from Subbaraya Sastri, son of Syama Sastri, and from the Anayya Brothers, great musicians of those days. Her mother Sundaramma learnt music from her mother and also from Annaswamy Sastri, the adopted son of Subbaraya Sastri. In each generation of the family, there had thus been the lateral transfusion of music from impeccable sources and, down each generation, the family wealth of music had been handed down as a precious heritage.

Dhanammal's training in music was initiated by family members themselves, among them her gramdmother Kamakshi. It is only later she became a sishya of gurus from outside the family fold.

The first such guru was a Vainika named Azhagasingarayya, who belonged to the sect of 'sathada' Vaishnavas that prepared flowers for temples. The compositions of the Sastriar mould, with their exquisite bhaava and intricate laya, suited Dhanammal's own bani.

Dhanammal knew many compositions of Tyagaraja's direct disciple Veena Kuppiar and of his son Tiruvotriyur Tyagier. The latter also known as Muthialpet Tyagier, was a great friend and admirer of Dhanammal, many years his junior.

Dhanammal was perhaps the first musician of repute who render Ettayapuram Kumara Ettendra's compositions, all first unveild in Subbarama Dikshitar's Sangeeta Sampradaaya Pradarsini.

Padas and Jaavalis were Dhanammal's forte. The principal source for her collection of padas which would have made a centipede proud was her teacher Balakrishna Das of Wallajapt, also known as 'padam' Baldas. He was a disciple of Mylapore Gowri Ammal, not the legendary dance exponent but a Veena vidushi.

Dhanammal's pursuit was more in the line of interpretation than creative art, strictly so called .... This was possible for her, because, by her long experience and vaste variety of musical assimilation. She was able to get at the core of each raaga and visualise its numerous facets as crystallised in the compositions of the old masters, which she lost no opportunity of learning. That is why every one of her aalaapanas presented a new feature of the same raaga and her exposition was always characterized by a perpetual freshness and individuality.

That is also the reason why her renderings were free from monotony and were not overweighted with uncouth expressions which conceal rather than express the peculiar characteristics of every raaga .... Her keen perception of the melodic individuality of different types of compositions and currect understanding of the peculiar merits of the different vaaggeyakaras and above all her right appreciation of the varying degrees of response of her instrument to the special characteristics of each class of composers were clearly noticeable in her expositions .... She exploited all the possibilities of the (Veena) to the fullest extent in rendering the grand sweeps of (Dikshitar) and intriguing curves.

Dhanammal was extremely sensitive to the minutest difference of pitch and the scrupulous care with which she tuned the Veena was an example to all musicians. The number of meettus she employed for a sanchaara was the minimum possible, and few equalled her in softness and delicacy of touch. The most commendable quality in her was the strict economy in the choice and use of phrases and embellishments. She always presented the core, the very soul of melody, the quintessence of music. Another characteristic of her art was her fidelity to classical traditions. Her music was the ecstatic out-pouring of a heart that felt and a mind that knew true beauty in sense and sound.

Emani Sankara Sastri

Emani Sankara Sastri was an artiste of outstanding distinctions—a Vainika, a researcher, a composer, a conductor and a teacher, for he always engaged in enhancing the appeal of music through his innovative technique. Emani Sankara Sastri born in Draksharamam (East Godavari) in 1922 was initiated into music at the very early age of 3. He gave his first performance in 1940 to a large appreciable audience. Because of his association with Diwan Bhahadur Naidu he was introduced to both Western and Hindustani music also.

According to him, "It is my conviction that all types of music can be played on the Veena. Once rapport with the instrument is established it responses to the players touch". He had superb control over the instruments that he brought out the sound potential-tonal colour on the Veena.

Emani did not use a pluck drum for playing, instead he used his nails. He was the first to use a contact mike.

His delineation of the raagas contained new elements fashioned by his own musical perception and creativity combined with novelty.

On the usage of gamakas—dasavidha gamakas he is of the opinion that they are inseparable which decorate the each musical phrase with precision. The same variety of gamaka appears with a different degree of intensity, tempo and range.

His music always envelopes spirituality synthesising tonality beauty and strength. He never trys to impress his listeners, he overwhelms them. On his orchestration technique its infinite range of expression and colour appeals to the imagination of music loving public. The concept or raaga and taala of Carnatic music has got a potential and can be thoughtfully composed to impressive orchestration.

(He was also a great teacher who trained a number of Vainikas like Chittibabu, M.Y. Kamasastry and a host of others).

His orchestration had an art of arranging the notes of a composition among the instruments of the orchestra and determined to a great extent the kind of melodies that he was supposed to use, he always kept in mind the characteristic sound of each instrument its range, the tonal quality. Thereby he was able to use in his orchestration a different families of musical instruments together.

As a versatile Vainika who reached a new dimensions and fulfilled the different tastes of all classes of audience and thereby adoring their hearts. He was a humble respecter of tradition yet was not so conservative on innovative ideas. His style accepted and blended all systems of music. He was equally well-informed of Hindustani, Western and Carnatic music.

He was a man of genius. This is evident from his introducing a totally new technique of fingering, plucking, simultaneous tones, tonal effect of strings etc. His absorption and involvement was remarkable. He was never conscious of the presence of audience and enjoyed each phrase in detail.

There is no doubt that he will continue to be honoured by future generations and the present alike.

Devakottai Narayana Iyengar

Born in 1905 at Devakkottai started his training in Veena at the very early age with Gottuvadyam Sakararamana and later on with the Karaikudi Brothers. He is known for his mastery in Manodharma aspect and established a name of his own. His music is notable for a medium tempo with brisk svara patterns without affecting the raaga bhaava.

He has served as the faculty member with the Central College of Music (Madras), Bharathiya Art Society (Bombay), Music Academy, (Madras), etc. Among his awards 'Kalaimamani', 'Central Sangeet Natak Akademi', 'Presidency Award', 'Mathurakala Praveena' are notable.

7

EXPONENTS OF CONTEMPORARY TRADITION AND STYLES

A. Questionnaire

In order to directly meet the contemporary Vainikas and ascertain their direct views on the very existence of a respective style or a school or a tradition to which they belong a Questionnaire was prepared.

Several Vainikas were interviewed in person by me and their views and the significance of their own style was ascertained from themselves. To maintain a uniform pattern of interview the following format of the Questionnaire was prepared and the interview was recorded for future reference. The discussion maintained in individual reference to most of Vainikas in this chapter is based on the facts obtained through this interview and also through printed sources where the interview could not be held.

Questionnaire

1. Biographical sketch :

   Family background, Parentage

2. How did your initiation to learning Veena take place? Whether by

   (a) Fascination

   (b) Serious attitude

(c) Traditional training

3. How many years of training you had?
   Is your style exactly on the lines of your guru?
4. Has any originality being added to later on to your technique.
5. Do you maintain, in your application the same trend both as learner-cum-teacher, as a teacher-cum-performer.
6. Is there any significant feature in your technical application?
7. In other styles of the Vainikas such as Karaikudi, Mysore, Thanjavur, etc. is there any special striking aspect that has inspired you?
8. What are the general difficulties that you face in adopting the same or different techniques as a learner, teacher and a performer?
9. While teaching students what are the main methodology that you adhere?
10. How do you visualise the audiences' response?
11. Do you attach equal importance for the manodharma and kalpitha aspect? Which is the area that you specialize?
12. Does all your concerts achieve a totality?
13. Whether you give equal importance to the Saahitya of a composition when you render it in the instrument?
14. Which tempo do you prefer in your rendering?
15. What is your preference of the different taanas?
16. How do you master the 'Kalapramana' of a song while learning it?
17. Do you recommend a continuous and easy rendering of a song in different 'Kalapramana'?
18. How far does the basic swara exercised help your achievement?
19. Just as 'akarasaadhakam' is prescribed for vocal which is the similar basic aspect recommended in Veena?

20. What is your opinion about contact mike in a public concert?
21. Do you approve learning by taped lessons?
22. How far does it help a student in his perfection?
23. How do you explain the utility of notation?
24. Is it possible to notate a particular phrase in a Krithi to make the students understand it easier?
25. What is the importance of taala strings and its usage in taanam?
26. In raaga aalaapana do you use the taala strings?
27. Do you agree that the tiny metalic pegs are steadier than the usual wooden-pegs?
28. Because of the usage of such metal objects, does it affect the tonal quality?
29. How do you reckon the different taalas like mishra-chaapu, kanda-chaapu, matya-taala, etc.?
30. How do you illustrate the changing course of 'gathi' pattern of mishra, kanda, etc...?
31. What is the ideal method suited for Pallavi exposition in Veena?
32. On the 'jathi' syllables (solkattu) is any special method adopted to bring out the identity of the 'jathi' with the help of the right hand?
33. Do you agree that a Vainika should also be a vocalist?
34. Do you rationalise Western aspects in your rendering? Is it merely to attract Non-Indian audience?
35. How do you rate the acoustics in Indian auditoriums compared with the acoustically balanced auditoriums of the West?
36. As a performer how do you satisfy the ideology of even a lay audience in your concerts?
37. Do you have the knowledge of any other similar instrument? Do you find opportunities to incorporate the technique of that instrument in your professional Veena?

B. Exponents

1. S. Balachandar

The lilting scintillating sounds of "Two-stringed-Musical-Instruments" of India have been responsible for spreading our "Indian-Classical-Music" literally throughout the length and breadth of 'Both-the-Hemispheres'. Thus it is that 'Sitar-Maestro' Ravi Shankar and 'Veena-Virtuoso' S. Balachandar are duly unanimously acclaimed as the "Pioneers" to have propagated the values of our Indian-Classical-Music all over the world, Ravi Shankar promoting the romantic raagas of "Hindustani" music through his bewitching 'Sitar' and Balachandar promulgating the divine-heritage of 'Carnatic' music through his soulful Veena.

Having had no Guru, totally unaided and untutored, Balachandar evolved and created a new-technique of Veena-playing (as he says: 'Entirely due to the bountiful blessings of The Almighty') which is a very difficult approach totally based on vocal-style. And thus, as the worthy innovator of an entirely new-style, new-school and new-system of Veena playing, Balachandar has established what is now known and referred to as 'Balachandar's style of Veena-playing' or as 'Balachandar's Veena bhaani' considered to be hitherto unknown, unexcelled and unparalleled and thus, may be, something even 'unattempted' before.

This he immediately did and in the year 1943 Balachandar performed his inaugural concert on the Veena in Madras and since then, leaving off playing on any other instrument, he has totally and completely dedicated himself to the Veena and Veena alone, heart and soul. He strictly adheres to traditional classicism. Any raaga he renders is soaked in aesthetic purity. He indeed is a Musicians' Musician. His music elevates the soul, with sublime sanctity. Balachandar now an 'International-celebrity' has won innumerable and unprecedented awards, honours and titles, amongst which are : 'Padma Bhushan' awarded by the President of India, the Sangeet-Natak-Akademi award in 1977, the Madras State Sangeetha Nataka Sangam title 'Kalaa-Sikhaamani' in 1968, 'Tantri-Vilas' awarded by Sur-Singar Samsad, Bombay in 1971,

'Sangeetha Chakravarthi' in New York, 'Veena Vaadya Saagarma' in London, 'Veenai Chemmal' in Singapore and 'Veena Varaprasaadi', 'Veena Chakravarti', 'Veena Yogi', 'Naada-Yogi', 'Naada-Brahmmam', 'Raaga-Brahmmam', 'Veena Praveena', 'Veena Marthaanda', 'Vainika Saamraat', 'Vainika Swayambhu', 'Vainika Siromani' etc. and thus Balachandar and Veena have become synonymous with one another. In the annals of Gramophone-Discs 'Recording-History' in our country, Balachandar has established yet another unprecedented 'Record'. Till date (26-2-1982), Balachandar has so far performed the maximum of 25 long playing records, which is the highest number of L.P. records performed by any Indian Classical Musician.

Amongst the 25 above-mentioned records, some deserve special and significant focus of attention. In a set of 12 Albums (Twelve L.P. Stereo Records), Balachandar has rendered (in the form of Extempore Melodic Improvisation) all the 72 melakarta raagas, which are the basic, fundamental root-raagas (parent scales) of Indian Classical Music. Out of these 72 melakarta (parent) raagas, hundreds and thousands of other raagas are born and derived. Balachandar's rendering of all the 72 melakarta raagas is verily hailed and acclaimed as a monumental historical musical offering of eternal value. To musicians, to musicologists, to music institutions, to music students, to music lovers all over the world, these 72 melakarta records performed by Balachandar will act as a permanent guide, reference, lexicon and melodic-dictionary. In his own words, Balachandar refers to these 72 melakarta records as his immortal legacy to musical posterity.

2. Chitti Babu

No genealogy trait in his line, he says, he is the only Veena player in his family like Mali (flute). His father—a Zamindar was the root cause for his developing interest in Veena. His father had a passion for learning. Chitti Babu, has inherited not a tradition but a gift which his father bequeathed by forcing him to develop the seed of interest to learn Veena at the very early age of 4 or 5 itself. More than his father's thrust upon him to learn Veena, he has made him play 'Vara Veena Mridu Pani-Mohana Geetham' in a correct form to clarify the incorrect form played by some one guest in his house when Chitti Babu was just 4 years old.

Later, he learnt under Pandravadu Mathiah, Iyuni Appalacharlu for some times before he became a regular disciple of Emani Shankara Sastri for about 6 to 7 years till he was 12. He started giving stage performance even then itself. He came to Vijayawada, as an artiste, with his Guru's training, in full-fledged form.

Again as it conveys in the interview held between the researcher and the artiste, he admits, there is no actual tradition to say, but his students are innumerable among whom, he mentioned some few like, Prabhavathi Ganesh, Sundar, Shanthi Rao, Suna Sudhindra and so on. Though his students are good enough in receptivity and adopting his style, he says due to lack of time, and other factors they are not able to advance as expected by him. His children took up to various other profession.

Recalling his good olden days, childhood experiences, when he was in his practising stage he says since his father was very strict to the core, even 999 times have practised, if one small error occured, his father used to insist and punish him, until he would play all the 1000 times with perfection by asking him to repeat the number of exercises from the beginning. This severe strictness has, he feels, helped him and stood him at good stead that today he has won an international reputation with his Divine Instrument. He sincerely owes to his Guru and his father for such a training given at that age.

As a performer, naturally, he is inclined more for Manodharma his special liking is raaga aalaapana, more so, the taanam also. Asked whether he pre-plans for his concerts, he says, it depends more on his moods and on the day's audience's response. He says, his main aim as a performer is to make his audience full justice in giving satisfaction for which, some times he may even have to change the mood of his approach. Since, he has extensively travelled abroad to (international) continents he has to see to the taste to his audience and play his items. Whether a heavy raaga in a heavy piece, or a lighter raaga in lighter vein, it does not matter, but he as an artist should and always must remember the duty to make his audience spell bound in his concert.

Asked about the tempo of a Krithi, he says each Krithi is set in a particular tempo already by Trinity and composers and it is always advisable to play in that set tempo. For example if 'Mokshamu Galada' is played in fast tempo (it cannot be obviously!) it surely will lose the charm and depth. It will become a laughing stock. So also, if a madhyamakaala Krithi is played in extreme vilambitam, the beauty is lost. However, for him his preference is more for madhyamakaala, and medium fast tempo Krithis, since it appeals even for lay people in the concert-hall. He stresses the importance of learning heavy pieces and handling pallavis and other tougher ones for literate audience who will cherish. A performer should know these tactics to attain success and acclamation.

He favours totally the idea of a contact mike and electronic mikes, which help to bring about a rich total colour adding more intensity and clarity to the pieces played, he advices a better sound system regarding our mike and amplifiers. Having used to a undoubtedly excellent system of acoustics abroad, where such perfection is given for every minutest detail in providing mikes, he cherishes the same while feels bad about the very poor acoustics in some of our concert halls. So according to him, contact mike, now-a-days is a boon for Veena artists in general. But in its application one should know as to how to control its volume. It should neither be too loud, lest the Vaadya will sound like a Raakshasa Veena nor should it be so feeble that its purpose is lost.

As for taped lessons, except for students from abroad, who are totally dedicated sincerely and who practice for many hours regularly, it is advisable to avoid giving to students from next door, lazily forgetting even single line taught. It will be even harmful to such unworthy students to train with taped lessons, since they never improve their Manodharma. It becomes poisonous and mechanical, hence, Chitti Babu is against this idea of taped lessons. At the same time he openly confesses that even after becoming to prank Vainika or artiste one can and should appreciate and learn whatever is good and musical in others. This approach is highly lofty, applaudable and to be welcomed by all music-lovers, so that it is the secret of our music to survive. Such a broad outlook mingled with good melodious Veena music is a gift from Almighty to Chitti Babu.

To him, just as to many other Vainikas, the Taala strings are mainly meant for taala production. A Veena is never complete, if taala strings are not used at its timely intervals as filled in a Krithi. Though violin is without taala strings, Kaalapramana is maintained. Whereas in Gottu Vaadyam taalam is used; why not in Veena. Why this biased view that it is more for decoration or drone? is his question. In fact, every beat in our music symbolises a taala, it has to be certainly reckoned. For aadi taala beat 1, 5, 7 should be reckoned. So also Rupakam 1, 2 beat should be properly and sensibly used for taala. Mishra chaapu and Kanda chaapu—the beat wherever occurs has to imply a taala, the taala strings serve as drone only in raaga aalaapana and taanam where it is for enriching beauty.

He remembers one good Vainika Veena Raghava Iyengar for his skill in gati laya patterns which paved way for his imbibing an interest to play both svara laghu and cross rhythmic svara kalpanas suitable for madhyamakaala Krithis. Again a final stress was laid by the artist, to see that as a performer, each one should strive hard to bring out both gaana rasam and bhaava rasam. Without bhaava our music is 'dead' he says. Hence, he chooses more of Tyagaraja Krithis for this aspect. One should have a basic knowledge about Telugu to understand Tyagaraja Krithis which are essence of Bhakti Bhaava. Quoted 'Sukhi Evvaro' where the pada garbham should occur.

Finally to sum up, his interview regarding the subject matter, it is better to recall his valuable quotation which he gave in Telugu, the purport translated in simple English given below.

"The artist however much he/she might have acquired knowledge in the field of music, can and does play or sing only up to one's limitations, cannot exceed this limit. A Vainika can play only to this limit of his abilities. Whereas he/she cannot play to the fullest limits of the Veena. He is restricted with his own limits just as a person filling his container in an ocean, not the full ocean itself but what it can hold only!"

Another beautiful quotation which he remembered and shared is worth mentionable.

"An art without industry is crime."

"An industry without art is brutality."

So humorously, yet with such clarity he distinguishes the 3 categories of artists.

1. One who plays not knowing as to why and how to appeal to audience.
2. One who cares for his audience.
3. One who cares just for his own personal happiness.

Hence it is highlight of his interview which helps us in the long run to cherish and inculcate, these advises.

His new area of a development he himself noticed in his Veena, is a blending of harmony with melody in our system of music though he does not say, he invented. It is a research after pretty years of service in this field, he discovered to his surprise. When Nyasa is done in Antara Gandhara, and reckoning of taala in s p s, gives an effect S, g, p, S which is both melody and harmony blended in our own music. Everyone can observe and try this, he says. Just as his great fascination for learning Veena was a right cause and nothing else, he admits it is his fancy to have tried to imitate 'koyil' voice which has now fetched him such world wide fascination and congrats.

One more noteworthy feature in him is, though he followed his guru's Mahamahopadhyaya Poojya Sri Emani Sankara Sastri in every respect, he confesses for his own introduction of originality. Every artist consciously or unconsciously develops a kind of originality along with adaptation of Guru's style. He says for a fine art like Veena, creativity and originality is a must.

3. Doreswamy Iyengar

Dr. V. Doreswamy Iyengar stands today as a fine example of the belief that when a person does sincerely what he enjoys most and allows his art to evolve from an inner sublimity, fame and honours seek him sooner or later.

Honours have come to Doreswamy Iyengar without his seeking them and the decolte and Padma Bhushan that have been awarded to him rest lightly on his shoulders.

It is easy to perceive Iyengar's passion for the Veena which he knows as the Queen of South Indian instruments. It is a dignified instrument which can only be enjoyed connoisseurs to refined taste. Its areas of strengths are its soft tonal quality and its capacity to produce the ten different types of graces or gamakas with fidelity. It may not be possible to play sustained **akaras** on the Veena, but Iyengar holds that its tone is akin to the lyrical speech of a baby whose sweet words and laughter have a greater impact on the listeners than the learned monologues of pandits. So much can be conveyed through a little Veena playing that it goes straight to the listener's heart. Quarter tones can be accurately reproduced. Take for instance, the gaandhaara of varaali, the rishabha of gowla, the gaandhaara of kalyani or the nishaadha of bhairavi; he says and observes. Their purity in the Veena is unparalleled. The Veena can produce certain graces and nuances close to the human voice.

Doreswamy Iyengar has been playing the Veena for more than five decades and his music has stood the test of time. It has grown and gained in richness and stature and today it stands like a banyan tree spreading its shade over a wide area, drawing deeply from the roots of tradition and giving free expression to the branches of manodharma but in conformity with the dictates of aesthetics. He has been blessed.

He was born in Gaddavalli in Hassan district in 1920 to Venkatesha Iyengar and Sringaramma. Venkatesha Iyengar was primarily a Veena player but after listening to Palladam Sanjeeva Rao's flute, he took a fancy to learning the flute and acquired proficiency in it. He later became a flutist in the Vidwans Orchestra at the palace, whose leader was Vainika Venkatagiriappa. Being friends and colleagues in the palace, the two vidwans had daily contact and used to visit each other's houses frequently. Venkatagiriappa was also Venkatesha Iyengar's guru at advanced levels of Veena playing.

He was seven when he came under the Venkatagiriappa who was strict disciplinarian. The master-student relationship was of the traditional variety and it elicited under monstrative affection from the former and humility, respect and devotion from the latter. Many hours were spend by the boy each day at the guru's house, absorbing and thriving in the world of music. Doreswamy Iyengar recalls that he had the ever present fear of being caned by his father guru. Without fail he put in the stipulated three hours of practice, including tikalasadhate (practice in three tempos) of all the primary lessons, at his guru's house every morning beginning at half-past six. Not only practising on the instrument but learning the text of Krithis and singing with the Veena was obligatory. Doreswamy sang while playing the Veena until the age of about sixteen when his voice broke.

Venkatagiriappa used to visit that the meettu or plucking must be done just to ensure that the twang of the string or the sound of wood would not be heard.

All through, he insisted that Veena playing should not be rough and difficult. There was no need to put in more effort than needed. The required effect must come easily without obvious strain to the performer. After Iyengar attained a high level of proficiency, he also taught him the cutcheri pattern with alternative playing by the two, but said raaga aalaapana and swaraprastaara should not be taught but should evolve by themselves. He widened his student's repertoire extensively, all the time correcting and perfecting the pieces already learnt. But throughout the period he taught Doreswamy, Venkatagiriappa protected him from over-praise and adulation least the youngster should fizzle out like a nine-day wonder.

The atmosphere was nourishing not only in his father's home and his guru's house but also in the country the 'Princely State' in which they lived. For the reign of Krishna Rajendra Wodeyar 4 in the first half of this century saw a revival and efflorescene of the fine arts in Mysore State which was held to be a model state in many other spheres too. The Maharajah had a cultivated and generous mind and the capacity to attract, befriend and retain a galaxy of musical talent to those times.

The Mysore Vainikas of the stature of Seshanna, Subbanna and Venkatagiriappa carved a niche for themselves by developing the unique instrumental potential of the Veena. In their solos and their roles in the Vidwans Orchestra, they did not restrict themselves to playing the Veena in the gayaki or vocal style. This was because in their opinion, that would be limiting the potential of the Veena. The raaga aalaapana and the Krithis were mostly rendered in the gayaki style, while their taanam, kalpana swaras and niraval had embellishments and added peep due to the employment of purely instrumental passages. These playing, and were not used all the time.

Iyengar identifies bhakti, saadhanaa and Veenaya-devotion, diligent practice and deep humility as the three essential requisite for attaining excellence in Carnatic music. In a way these are the qualities which form the substratum out of which his music flows to the delight of all.

Doreswamy Iyengar's music is a judicious blend of vocal and instrumental technique. His exposition of raagas has been highly enjoyable and edifying. His delicate ornamentation in many desya raagas have an underlying appeal.

4. E. Gayatri

Starting at the very age of 5, she followed the tradition of her mother Kamala who was a disciple of 'Kalpakam Swaminathan' and the stalwarts of 'Kalaksetra'. Her first performance was in the 9th year. Based on an interview, the researcher was able to elicit her various experiences and views on varied subjects on the tradition of Veena. Such as:

1. She could not identify any particular school or paani having influenced on her playing technique.
2. Her desire to become a professional and serious performing artist had taken a deep route at the very perfomance.
3. Her total training in Veena, spanned from 5th to 9th year.
4. She emphatically opined on the essential knowledge of vocal technique.

5. For learning purposes she does not advocate the help of notation.
6. For beginners, she adds that learning through recorded music will be highly damaging. On the contrary experienced performers can fully take the advantage of such medium.
7. Practice of basic and pedagogical lessons is a must for any performer or teacher irrespective of his/her age. This even today is followed by Srimati Gayatri.
8. On the concert pattern, she adjusts to satisfy both the connoisseurs and lay public alike by selecting classical pieces of heavy and light nature without sacrificing its classical bias.
9. Likewise, even the tempo-swaras and compositions—of all types is maintained throughout to avoid monotony.
10. At the same time, she expressed her dislike to the importance given to concert-gimmicks, by professionals (including herself) for mass appeal.
11. As a performer and a teacher she does not believe in making a compromise on the strength or standard of pieces.
12. On the quality of the instrument *vis-a-vis* on the standard she believes in the conventional Veena leave alone the fibre glass or dismantable Veena.
13. On her technique, she believes that the identity is because of her continuous vibration and sound given for each and every detailed of a note. The gamakas though described in the Lakshana gandas are not the only once played on the instrument, but several and innumerable unidentifiable tones are also audible in the production of the technique.
14. This specialisation of her technique with importance to gamaka has forced her to take the help of the contact mike so as to make eligible even the minutest sound more audible to pre-lessoners.
15. She distinguishes her technique of building a continuity among gones as her special feature.

16. On the technique of the playing the pallavi, she expressed her aversion to sing the saahitya part for the listeners since from her point of view this approach makes one's attempt incomplete.

Her open minded approach and inspiration from several contemporary Vainikas was visible during the short interview the researcher had with Gayatri.

5. Kalpakam Swaminathan

She had her early training from her mother who was a traditional artist of high classicism. She also learnt violin and hormonium and advanced coaching from Anantha Krishna Iyer, who was a descendant of Dikshitar family and Budalur Krishnamurthy Sastri. Even at the very early age she had the talent to play difficult raagas like 'Vagadiswari' etc. It is highly remarkable to know that she had also taken a fancy to play a varnam or a Krithi in a tambura with the aid of a movable object for fret.

She is always of the opinion that learning becomes complete more through listening and infusing on oneself the creative originality within. She gives an equal importance to the vocal technique or saahitya Bhaava in her rendering. About Kaopithe Sangita she considers that no special training is necessary or in other words it has to be learnt on their own.

On learning a Krithi she emphasises both the dhaatu and matu of each and every line of the composition—be it the pallavi or the anupallavi or the charana or the end portion of charana—must be thoroughly learnt.

On the teaching methods her mode of approach is in line with the accepted convention practised in a gurukula system. She used to select and teach songs that could be easily understood and learnt according to the individual capacity calibre of the disciple. To be more precise she also makes it a point in adopting innovative teaching of basic swaraavali exercises in the same avartha in different variations of speed. The same set of disciples are also taught varnams in heavy and major raagas like Thodi,

Shankaaraabarana, etc. For playing the second speed of the varnams she insists on the same fingering method. Another technique that she adopts is the initial teaching of the svara placements in the same fret and later on the placement of the svara being shifted to the preceding fret by inflecting that particular string. For example *ri in sa, ma* in *aga, da* in *pa, sa* in *ni* etc.

Even while teaching fingering technique she adopts different methods according to the calibre of the disciple. Like a true traditional vocalist Kalpakam Swaminathan insists on padaccheda of the Saahitya while executing the song through the Veena.

She opines that :

(*a*) It takes at least 12-15 years to become intellectually matured Vainika.

(*b*) Her guru used to get irritated if any of her/his disciples interrupt with any question of academic nature. The disciple was expected of to learn only what has been taught to them.

(*c*) So Kalpakam Swaminathan encourages and insists on her disciples to be more inquisitive and become master Vainikas with more information and clarification on what one is going to play or learn.

In her concerts she has no special preference for selecting a particular raaga. Moresoever she does not give any weightage to the mass appeal. But she prefers to select rare and lesser known raagas for Radio concerts.

Her influence of style is sanchaaries, visible in Gayatri's rendering whose mother also learnt under Kalpakam Swaminathan.

On the question of reckoning taala she insists that for each beat the taala must be markedly played.

Unnecessary meettus must be avoided in the middle of a Krithi to avoid confusion as to whether it is a taala or a decoration. Whereas in taanam the taala strings serve as drone and ornamental. Hence she reckons taala strings only on beats logically which seems sound and aggreeable. In each variety of taala in a Krithi she uses taala strings only for taala purpose and no intermediate meettus are heard.

6. K.S. Narayanaswamy

Born in 1914 in Kerala he received intensive training with his parents Sivarama Iyer and Narayaniammal and his brother K.S. Krishnayyar. At the very early age of seven he gave his first public performance.

The pursuit of music for him is a continuous search to find out the sampradaaya. As a true traditionalist he represents the quintessence of Carnatic tradition—a tradition of laws and doctrines evolved over several centuries. He represents the accumulated heritage and the creavitity of many great Vainikas with a high perception. He has been a major force of creativity. His method of playing technique is known for its ease and mellifluous flow with a scientific approach.

He was on the staff of Annamalai University, Swati Thirunal Music Academy at Tiruvanantapuram and Shanmugananda Sangeeta Vidyalaya at Bombay. Among his numerous awards, the Academy awards of Kerala and Tamilnadu, Sangeeta Kalaanidhi and the prestigeous Padma Bhushan are noteworthy.

7. R. Pichumani

Born on May 18, 1920, R. Pichumani hails from a family of musicians. After profiting by early training at the age of 10 in vocal music from Jalar Gopala Aiyar, he later took to the Veena and underwent discipleship under Tiruchi Kupanna. He was 15 by the time and had already established his talents by winning the prestigeous award of the National College, Tiruchi in a Carnatic vocal music content.

Studying up to the S.S.L.C. in the National College School he later joined the Annamalai University and became a Sangeeta Bhushanam in Veena after completing the four years course leading to it very successfully.

In no hurry a concert career, he started for it only after he was convinced, he was mature enough and quite quipped for it. This phase of his life started from his 20th year after a period of intensive study in the University under stalwarts like Tiger Varadachariar, K.S. Narayanaswami Aiyar and V.S. Gomathi Sankara Aiyar.

His pursuit of Veena music has been dedicated to traditional values and for the past four decades he has enjoyed a steady and dignified professional career during which, apart from conventional success, recognition of his merit and his services to music have come in the form of honours and titles.

Embanking on a professional career in 1940, he has given over 1,500 performances till date and these include public concert performances, radio programmes (including the prestigeous National Programme and Sangeeta Sammelan Programmes), T.V. appearances etc. He had been awarded Top Rank Artiste by All India Radio.

His participation in the Madras Music Academy festivals have covered both main performing assignments and demonstrations. He is the recipient of 'Shanmuga Vadivu' award twice from the Academy.

Among the important awards are the 'Kalaimamani' title and Gold Medal conferred on him by the Tamil Nadu Iyal Isai Nataka Manram in 1970-71, and Veena Nadu Mani in 1982 by His Holiness Sri Sankarachariar of Kanchi Kamakoti Peetam and President award by Sangeeta Natak Akademi, New Delhi.

He has had occasion to serve as Secretary of the Thiruvaiyar Thyaga Brahmotsavam in 1980.

The Tamil Nadu Government has utilised his services to serve on the selection board for appointing staff to the State Music Colleges and a Chief Examiner for the final examinations of the Vidwan courses.

Annamalai University has appointed him as one of the members in the Faculty of Arts and the Board member of practical Examination Committee.

In 1969, the Central Sangeeta Natak Akademi took two hour recording of his Veena music for preservation in the Central Archives. The Gramophone Company (Columbia) has recorded many 78 R.P.M. Records and L.P. Records and Audio Cassette by A.V.M. His raaga playing is noted for its purity and traditional values.

He has trained many disciples who are successful performing artists.

He has composed swara jatis, Varnam, Jaawalis and invented a new raaga Vasantha Kaisiki and a jaavali in the same raaga janya from the 16th Mela.

He has trained his two musically talented sons—P. Viswananthan who is the staff guitarist of All India Radio, Madras is the exponent of Classical and Western Music. Viswanathan also plays the Mridangam and Santoor; P. Chandrasekaran who is a professional Veena player gives performances individually and also accompanies his father R. Pichumani.

8. Rajeswari Padmanabhan

Born in 1939. Hailing from the Karaikudi family. She has inherited the family heritage of the Veena from Karaikudi Sambasiva Iyer. Her added asset of being able to sing along the Veena. Her playing is imbibed with the maturity of the final aspects of the Karaikudi Brothers. She has also learnt music from Mysore Vasudevachar. Her strict adherence to classical forms, musical phrasing and pace displays her traditional maturity. Her music is full of clarity, emphasising a sedate tempo of high order. Her taanam is also excellent with clear meettu producing harmony of rare excellence.

She is attached to the faculty of the famous Kalakshetra institution and her award include 'Kalaimaamani' and 'Central Sangeet Natak Akademi Awards'.

9. Ranganayaki Rajagopalan

Born in 1932. She has the unique distinction of having been with Karaikudi Sambasiva Iyer as a member of the family as well as his disciple. Today she represents the Karaikudi School of Veena. From the early age of 7, she started her first performance with her guru. She also acquired her repertoire through several vidwans who visited her house. Among her awards, the 'Kalaimaamani' and 'The Madras Music Academy Awards' are notable.

10. K.P. Sivanandham

Descending in the direct line of the traditional Vainika style of Thanjavur, Sri Sivanandham inherits a rich heritage for his merit.

An ardent disciple of Desamangalam Subramaniya Iyer (the then Professor of Annamalai University) Sri Sivanandham imbibed his guru's style in all respects. He had a refreshing coaching under Prof. Sabesa Iyer also. Pragmatic by temperament he stands for his methodical system of Veena learning.

Besides being a reputed Vainika, Shri Sivanandham is also known for his nattuvaangam, and a good composer himself of varied Krithis, darus, tillaanas and so on.

He believes strongly in a foundation course in vocal music for every Veena student at least for 5 to 6 years. This is in order to gain steadiness and clarity to become a good performer in Veena in a later stage. Her one will be surprised to know that he had a vocal training for himself for about 5 years, which has helped him, he feels, to know the rudiments of perfection in the art of Veena. Hence, he advocates more stress for every Vainika to be initially and preferably a vocalist.

Another major vital feature for which, much importance is laid in this particular style is the area of gamaka. When asked about initially of taala strings, Sri and Srimati Sivanandham, expressed their view, that, in a Veena, the taala strings serve much as a 'drone' than for mere taalam alone. They feel, most of the Vainikas overdo this taala strings, by over-lapping the main-strings affect, finally resulting in loosing the charm of the piece played. This is the main reason, they feel, the taala strings need not be used much in a Krithi or taanam unlike the other Vainika's styles. In their style, more stress is laid for raaga, bhaava, gamaka and sahitya meettu than the so-called technical gimmicks, as they title it. In order to save the purity and weight of the item played, the volume mingled with perfect shruti atonement is enough to render a piece with all success in its production.

Sri Sivanandham feels that there is no distinction as main or heavy raagas but what he likes as favourite raaga becomes his 'best'. Psychologically, every Vainika or artist gets a mastery over a particular raaga, depending on his/her taste.

The raaga aalaapana, Smt. and Sri Sivanandham feel, should immediately and readily bring out the clue for the piece which is going to be played successively. In other words, the raaga aalaapana forms a prelude as a key note, to the emerging Krithi of his choice in that raaga. Ex. (Birana Varilichi)—Kalyani—Rupakam

Regarding taanam part of Manodharma, not special importance is given by him. His choice seems to lie only on raaga aalaapana than rendering a taana, which has a fascination for other schools of Veena.

To them, no pre-preparation is undergone before performing a concert. He said, since it becomes monotony to prepare swara passages earlier and to avoid "mechanical output", and to differentiate the actual creative (Manodharma) aspect on the stage from already planned one, they do not have pre-preparation as elaborately done by some other styles of Veena. However, for attaining synchronization, within two Veenas, it is better to note down, the selection of item part of it. Manodharma, should spring forth, only on the stage depending on the artist's moods, which again depends on the "kind of audience present". He admits, the concerts sometimes failing in the expected percentage, due to the reason alone, where an artist loses his/her mood, if no receptivity or response is seen. This holds good with almost performer in general.

According to Sri Sivanandham, a Veena student gain perfect control over Kalapramanam, must—should attempt to learn at least 30 to 40 Krithis (heavy pieces of Muthuswamy Dikshitar) few slow-temposed padams of Kshetrangna, which implies a regular and strenuous practice to achieve this aim. After attainment, that particular student can shine as a performer without much difficulty. He says, he himself had learnt, practised many Dikshitar's Krithis and Kshetragna's padams in Chowka Kalam. They both feel, instead of attempting for 'rare raagas' in unacquainted areas, which have no depth for flavour as such, it is enough if our teachers, students and performer pay more attention to skillfully eke out the essence of raagas such as Kalyani, Kamboji, Todi, Shankarabharanam, etc. The rest of the attempts without any creative ability in these above-said raagas are but just 'futile and dry . He says, the audience come to concerts to forget their domestic worries, in listening to good concert, but it often happens, that many regretfully return without satisfaction because the performer does not care for producing effective Kalyani or Todi instead raagas of feebler veins with just jumble of svara passage thus not transforming or moulding the listener's soul.

Thus, the concert becomes "utter flop-failure" both to himself and to the audience. This is the reason why he lays stress on Todi, Kalyani than on fancy raagas like Revathy, etc.

In the playing technique, he feels, it is enough if (left hand) pulling gamaka exercises are well practised than right hand fingering—which is but mere 'gimmicks' in Veena art.

As for notation and taped lessons, they have aversion since, the technique becomes fully 'mechanical'. Notation can be given to the 'beginner' in music till varnam or so but not in an advanced stage. By then the student should have gained the valuable knowledge in the region of Manodharama.

Perfect still in all 3 sthaayis for a student right from his early stage is stressed by Sri Sivanandham. For performer he advocates the use of contact mikes to bring out karvai and nuances in pieces.

He served in the faculty of music at Annamalai University and later with the Carnatic College of Music, Madras. Among his awards 'Kalaimaamani', 'Sangeeta Sudhaamani', 'Veenai Vithagar' are noticeable, he has also authored the famous compositional works of the Thanjavur Quartet, his great great grand fathers.

His life-partner Srimati Sharada who hails from a family of musicians is an equally talented Vainika. She always accompanies the devoted Vainika Sri Sivanandham in all his concerts.

11. R.K. Suryanarayana

Coming from a very privileged lineage of dedicated artist R.K. Suryanarayana inherited the instrumental tradition from his father K.S. Kesavamurthy. As a child prodigy at the age of 7 he took vocal and Veena simultaneously. His base of artistry with old tradition and inimitable technique made him break new grounds in sound patterns of his instrument.

His music with theoretical dogmas with absolute sense of conviction has made an impact on the audience. His resourcefulness and the gliding ease of the fingers have become style of his own. Among his techniques the display of swaram even on the right hand bridge of the Veena where there are no help of frets and employing numerous such techniques is really praise-worthy. He uses all his fingers with amazing precision raising across the frets with incredible speed. With the spirit of classicism he can interweave intricate virtuosity with a harmonising effect.

The beauty of his handling the instrument while playing the fourth string brings out the lucidity of the saptha svaras is a great rare feature.

Wizard R.K. Suryanarayana who is synonymous with Veena and a multifaceted personality comes from a very privileged lineage of dedicated artists. His father mentor Asthaana Vidwan of erstwhile Mysore, R.S. Keshava Murthy, an interprid experimenter handed over the heirlom Veena to him which had come down for at least 300 years, known as 'Gayathri'. This instrument with seventeen additional strings to the seven the Veena has, are so arranged and fitted in order to enhance the sonority of the instrument, that reverberates when the usual strings are struck producing orchestral sounds.

Suryanarayan began his career as a vocalist at the age of seven. Hailed as a child-prodigy, he took up to Veena subsequently and is a legend today among his contemporaries. He bases his artistry on the inherited wealth of age-old tradition and his indomitable technique with no debt to any particular stylisation, impels him to break new ground in weaving new sound patterns of musical excellence, that casts a hypnotical spell on the audience. Thus, he is at once a connoisseurs' delight, a classicists dilemma and critics despair.

His music bound by theoretical dogmas interpreted with an absolute sense of conviction thus sustaining fluency and freedom in the midsts of classical constraints, is certainly an awe inspiring experience indeed! The starting variety of musical effects kaleidoscopic and lilting model pictures emerge from his infinite imagination and glow with the purest of classical effluence. In the Krithi rendition he has a definite fascination to the potent blend of emotion and orderliness that is instantaneously communicative to the audience who throng to his concert venues and thus he is able to ride on the wings of glory. It is remarkable how Suryanarayan with his unrivalled resourcefulness and phenomenal ease is able to maintain crescendo of velocity, unblemished and involuntary gliding of the fingers on the frets in the swara rhythms resembling a flood of musical patterns unleashed from his finger tips. One has to listen to believe his Thanamalika in harmonious blend of classicism and originality that cannot be dreamt of by the general run of Veena players.

Suryanarayan by his impressive presence and personal charm both as a Veena player and a conversationalist in many languages can give a learned exposition on the technique of his art. He is a veracious reader and his articles contributed to various journals have taken even the poet laureates by surprise.

Young as he is, he has already achieved march, has travelled widely both in India, and abroad including U.S.A., U.K., France, Canada, the Middle East and Japan. He has also toured extensively in South East Asia, Hong Kong and Philippines. He participated in the South of France. He gave a benefit performance at Ballore under the aegis of the Indo-Canadian Association for the Bangladesh Relief Funds. He also gave a charity recital at the London Centre of Bharatiya Vidya Bhavan.

Suryanarayan has been fortunate enough to achieve his ambitions having been acclaimed by high dignitaries, international organisations and recognitions by way of receiving titles and honours from leading music associations.

Kala Purna, Vainika Kula Chandra, Nada Jyothy, Veena Vadana Gandharva, Veena Chakravarthy, Vainika Shiromani, Isai Mannan, Ganamrutha Vainika, Isai Tendra, Vainika Thilaka, Vainika Vara Kesari, Veena Visharada, Vainika Shikhamani, Vainika Kantheerava, Bharatha Vainika Vidya Bhaskara, Bharatha Vainika Rathna, Veena Samrat, Veena Vidya Nidhi, Swara Samrat, Guru Seva Chatura, Gayathri Veena Vivasvantha, Veena Vittagar, Vainika Nada Durandhara, Karnataka Rajyotsava Award and Kalamaamani from Tamil Nadu. Recently, he has the distinguished honour of the coveted Asthaana Vidwan of Manthraalaya.

He is an authoritative composer and the compositions structurally cogent have been in wide circulation on concert stages.

12. T.N. Seshagopalan

Born at Nagapattinam to Sri Nambi Iyengar and Srimati Tiruvenkatavalli in 1948 Seshagopalan learnt music from the age of 7, from his mother and later with Madurakalpra Veena Sri C.S. Sankara Sivam who was the well-known disciple of Muthiah Bhagavathar and Poochi Iyengar. He is more popularly acclaimed as a top ranking vocalist of India and recently has added his acclaim as a Vainika also. He has widely travelled both in India and abroad. His audio credits include several discs and LPs. He has composed many tillanas in Hindustani and Carnatic raagas. Endowed with a rich voice and super natural creativity he has been able to capture rapt attention of millions of connoisseurs and lovers of music. His versatility is supreme—both in vocal and Veena in the exposition of the complete colour and picture of a raaga—be it popular or rare. Among his numerous Awards and Titles the most noteworthy is the conferment of the 'Asthaana Vidwan' title and the "Tiruppugazhmani" bestowed by H.H. Jayendra Saraswathi. Other titles are Sangita Choodamani, Gana

Bhubathy, Kalarathnam, Sangita Sudhakara, Gayaka Choodamani, Kalaimaamani, etc.

On the teaching-learning process for Veena students he is of the opinion that one must be taught most of the major raagas like Shankarabharanam, Thodi, Kalyani, etc. Every student must be made to learn any composition or a raaga aalaapana paddhathi from basic view to advanced level. The application of proper gamakas and meettus must be left to the student to improve upon.

His particular identification of the Veena technique is the complete utilization of the vocal rendering.

8

ANALYSIS OF THE STYLES OF CONTEMPORARY VAINIKAS

(Supportive Annexure for Audiography)

I have already mentioned in my introductory statement that I did listen to numerous live concerts of those Vainikas on whom I am now going to make an attempt in analysing their individual stylistic rendering. But still I found it very difficult in analysing the actual method of play by each Vainika in the absence of my directly listening to the liver performance and the exact mode of their reckoning the different technique on a closer orbit. Therefore, whatever I have discussed and analysed in this section are solely based on my sheer listening alone.

Every instrumentalist has his own ways of handling the instrument to produce and reflect his own style of presenting any format of music. In this respect the old as well as the present day masters of Veena adopted a distinctive and unique method of producing musical sounds—be it a song or a raaga or kalpana svaras or for that matter even the tempo of the composition. It must also be noted that the production of the volume of both the plucking and fingering varies from person to person.

With this guideline I have attempted to make a detailed analysis of the playing technique of the Vainikas whose rendering I have included in the illustrative portion as I have understood them. They are as follows:

1. K.S. Narayanaswamy (Thodi raaga and taanam)

He makes use of deep gamakas especially for gandhara in both madhya and thara sthaayi. For the pharase mpdp mpdp gmpn rn srqn a variety of twisted fingering are 'tripan' is frequently seen. While playing the taanam stress is given more for the meettu in alternate formation. In his rendering the second string is rarely used. So far as the composition analysed in this illustration is one mishra chaapu taala—here the artist gives two strokes for mishra chaapu taala (Takita + Taka Dhhmi) a common feature in use.

2. V. Doreswamy Iyengar (Purvikalyani—Devadeva—Rupakam and Mukhari—Entha ninne—Rupakam)

More display of swings and sways in a lower wait of the Purvi Kalayani raaga. In the higher range over shadow of notes are very explicitly produced. Some times notes without gamaka (or plain notes) are inter-woven with soft meet us. At many instance very soft but frequent meettus with jumps are noticeable from one sthaayi to next. Another technique that is visible is the frequent aestheticaly enjoyable twisted fingering (or Tripam). Unlike some other Vainikas the meettu is not abruptly stopped nor cut-short.

The second piece in Mukhaari was actually played after nearly a gap of two decades when the first along was played by him. There is lot of and immense difference in the tonal quality and the timbre of the notes produced in his music.

3. Chitti Babu (Kharaharapriya raaga and tanaam)

The most noteworthy aspect is the simultaneous and frequent plucking combined with fingering in two strings. Rare usage of tripan is heard. Expression of the direct application of scales is quite common. Another point of importance is the two or three meettus for a swara passage having several permutation.

(pdns rgrs ndpmgrs). The same method of playing is to be adopted for the taanam also and an elongant continuity is maintained. Another important variation is the unique style of chord progression.

(s g r m g p) He is more adept in utilising the higher (p d s) sthaayi. While playing taanam again we noticed the soft meettus and double notes in high speed.

Another most noteworthy and highly difficult concept is the display of the same set of svaras in two different strings, different frets and in two octaves simultaneously. For example.. ..

pdmSS mpdnSS
pdnSS mpdnSS ... ...

4. E. Gayatri (Pantuvaraali—Aparaamabakthi—Rupakam and Punnaagavaraali—folk songs)

An uncomparable feature of brisk and horizontal phrases are visible throughout her playing. Very light and unrecognisable stress and accent in plucking is her forte. Most of her playing is confined to higher octave range. Another visible aspect of reducing the longer duration of notes either by mere jerk or a stress is noticeable. Lot of maintaining continuity throughout looks like a breathless effort with high control over the instrument.

5. R. Pichumani (Raaga—Mohana—Rama ninnu namina—Adi)

His music is evident with more instances of purity. He specialises in bringing forth the touches of sober, sublime, soft, soothing, sensitive and sincerity.

6. Kalpakam Swaminathan (Kalyani-Raagam and Taanam)

A purely indigenous music with a conservative style of play — both fingering and meettus. Her unique touches in middle octave ranges are away from flamboyant style of play. She has a unique way of pesenting elongant strokes endowed with highly classical and traditional application of pure and opt gamakas. In all the three sthayis the flow of swara phrases are highly praise-worthy.

Even for taanam equal and consistent distribution of notes in all the three octaves with variations of speeds. Her nature of playing vividly portrays unassuming approach.

7. Emani Sankara Sastri (Raaga Karaharapriya and Tillaanaa in Behag)

His music which is quite different from conservative approaching but full of classicism. His style of playing is distinguishable as:

— Highly scintillating overtones with gracious and reverberating overtures;

— A unique style of producing vibrational tones full of esthetically pleasing micro tones;

— Even in his adoption of highly technical and non-conservative style, his clear expression of standard and accepted phrases and prayogas are highly appreciable phenomena;

— He makes full use of all the four strings thus covering all the five octaves; thereby gives a broader perspective and colour of the raaga;

— Even in lower range expression of frills, shakes and trills are clearly elaborated;

— The tillaanaa composition is full of specific, apt and speculate meettu technique.

8. T.N. Seshagopalan (Purvikalyani—Ananda Nadanamakriya—Rupakam—Nilakantha Sivan)

A unique mode of presenting highly classical and at the same time innovative way of mixing vocal and instrumental technique. The complete identity and colour to the raaga is fully portrayed with efficient expression of more articulate and appropriate gamakas. His mode of rendering is highly influenced with gamakas swara korvais of his indigenous style of vocal efficiency.

9. S. Balachandar (Shankarabharana raaga)

A unique system of presenting the structure and colour of a raaga through his own method of deflecting a particular swara to unimaginable length. In other words his way of expressing the sixth or seventh swara in the initial fret itself is highly praise-worthy and difficult task. Another point of interest is the soloist tempo adopted in presenting either a composition or a raaga or even a swara passage. This might probably be due to his awakening and painstaking effort to picturise the nadathma rupa of a particular raaga or its related aspects. His mode of fingering is also quite different from others *i.e.* he uses the method of applying the same finger for the same frets most of the time.

SUMMARY

To study this area of research, now I feel that one should have gained atleast not less than two decades of intensive training, coaching and guidance under a single teacher (Gurukula vasam) and the institutional system of training only will not be sufficient enough to make one realise and understand the intricacies of the instrument in general and the topic in particular.

In the forgone pages it gives an outline information of the individual Vainikas—medieval and contemporary period—who represented different schools of thought followed by a general focus on the tradition of concert in general spanning from ancient to the trinity period.

The discussion follows with more or less emphasis on the technique (Instrumental-Veena) involved with the handling of the instrument. For instance different types of meettus, plucking and fretting are introduced. The main study is based on the three major schools of Veens—Tanjore, Mysore and Andhra schools along with their distinguishing features.

A chronological and genealogical background of several Vainikas who lived in the 18th, 19th and the 20th century is also discussed. The study of the contemporary Vainikas include late S. Balachander, Chitti Babu, Dr. Mysore Doreswami Iyengar, E. Gayatri, Kalpakam Swaminathan, K.S. Narayanaswamy R. Pichumani, Rajeswari Padmanabhan, Ranganayaki Rajagopalan, K.P. Sivanandam etc.

Another crucial section on the individual veena playing is analysed and discussed focusing on atleast three major identical technique and style.

An elaborate study on many more Vainikas would be worthwhile for any further researchers to tread upon on the same lines.

INDEX